"*Opening the Door* provides practical steps that will help ministers integrate healthy relationships, biblical gender equality, and sanctity of life principles into their standard premarital counseling style."

Rev. Aleese Moore-Orbih
Evangelical Covenant Church

"This is the book on premarital counseling we need. If 25-50% of couples will experience violence in their relationships, pastors have an urgent responsibility to educate couples who come to the church for blessing of their marriages. If all pastors will follow the suggestions in this book, the church will begin to fulfill its responsibility for safety and holiness in Christian families."

Dr. James Newton Poling
Garrett-Evangelical Theological Seminary
Evanston, IL

"This is a long overdue and much needed resource for those of us who support and challenge couples to create healthy marriages…a theological and pastoral resource we all need."

Rev. Dr. Lucy Forster-Smith
Chaplain, Macalester College
St. Paul, MN

"Domestic violence awareness is an ethical necessity for those in helping professions. Susan Yarrow Morris provides a wonderful resource for pastors providing premarital counseling."

Dr. Cher N. Edwards
Seattle Pacific University

"Susan Yarrow Morris has developed a useful tool integrating premarital counseling with the difficult but pervasive issue of domestic violence. Morris provides important sociological, theological and biblical background on the nature of domestic violence and a theological perspective that pushes pastors to take it seriously in our work with couples before they are married."

Rev. David Kratz
Fauntleroy United Church of Christ
Seattle, WA

Opening the Door:

A Pastor's Guide to
Addressing Domestic Violence
in Premarital Counseling

Rev. Susan Yarrow Morris

In collaboration with

Jean Anton

Working together to end
sexual & domestic violence

www.faithtrustinstitute.org

Opening the Door: A Pastor's Guide to Addressing Domestic Violence in Premarital Counseling

Susan Yarrow Morris
In collaboration with Jean Anton

Working together to end
sexual & domestic violence

Seattle, WA
www.faithtrustinstitute.org

Copyright © 2006 FaithTrust Institute

All rights reserved. With the exception of the handouts on pages 72-89, no part of this publication may be reproduced in any manner without permission in writing from the publisher.

Permissions/Credits will be found on pages v-vi, which constitute an extension of the copyright page.

Design by Moonlight Design

ISBN No. 978-0-9745189-4-7

Printed in the United States of America

PERMISSIONS | CREDITS

The publisher sincerely thanks the following sources for permission to reprint copyrighted material. We have made every effort to acknowledge all sources from which quotations were copied or adapted. We apologize for any inadvertent errors or omissions on our part, and will correct them in future editions.

All Scriptural quotes, unless otherwise noted, are from *New Revised Standard Version Bible*, copyright 1989, Division of Christian Education of the National Council of the Churches of Christ in the United States of America. Used by permission. All rights reserved.

Hosea 12:6 quote adapted by author from *The Message*. Copyright 1993, 1994, 1995, 1996, 2000, 2001, 2002. Used by permission of NavPress Publishing Group.

Isaiah 61:1 from *United Church of Christ Book of Worship*, copyright 1986, United Church of Christ Office for Church Life and Leadership.

"Beyond What" from *Revolutionary Petunias & Other Poems*, copyright © 1973 and renewed 2001 by Alice Walker, reprinted by permission of Harcourt, Inc.

"A Third Body" reprinted from *Loving a Woman in Two Worlds*, HarperCollins, New York, 1987. Copyright 1987 Robert Bly. Used with permission of Robert Bly.

"The Conditions" by Bennie Lee Sinclair, from *The South Carolina Review*, Volume 34, #2, Spring, 2002. Reprinted with permission of *The South Carolina Review*.

Power & Control Wheel and Equality Wheel by permission of the Domestic Abuse Intervention Project, Duluth, Minnesota.

"Saving the Family: When is the Covenant Broken?" by Mitzi N. Eilts from *Violence Against Women and Children*, edited by Carol J. Adams and Marie M. Fortune. Reprinted by permission of the Continuum International Publishing Group.

"Indicators that a Man May Kill his Partner" and "Accountability" from "Assessing Whether Batterers Will Kill" by Barbara Hart, 1990. Reprinted with permission of the Pennsylvania Coalition Against Domestic Violence.

"Predictors of Domestic Violence" from *General Information Packet: Every Home a Safe Home*. Reprinted by permission of National Coalition Against Domestic Violence.

"A Community Checklist for Faith Communities." Reprinted by permission of Nebraska Domestic Violence Sexual Assault Coalition.

Excerpts from "Counseling the Clergy on How to Help Victims of Domestic Violence" by SaraKay Smullens, from *Annals of the American Psychotherapy Association*, November/December 2001. Reprinted with permission of the *Annals of the American Psychotherapy Association*.

A DEDICATION

With thanks to Marie M. Fortune, pioneer and friend;

With love to David M. Morris, covenant partner in life and work;

For Alexander and Jacob, beloved grandsons,
    with the hope that they and others who are yet young
        may know the joy of healthy covenantal relationships
            which offer safe dwelling and abundant life
                to body, mind and spirit.

SUSAN YARROW MORRIS
August, 2005

CONTENTS

Acknowledgments xi

Preface: Dear Colleague...A Letter of Concern and Challenge xiii

Chapter One: Introduction: Beginning With Us, the Pastors 1

Chapter Two: Biblical and Theological Foundations. 5

Chapter Three: What Every Pastor Needs to Know About Domestic Violence. 13

Chapter Four: Components of Premarital Counseling 21

Chapter Five: Addressing Domestic Violence in Premarital Counseling 29
                Part 1: Screening for domestic violence with individuals. 30
                Part 2: Educating couples about domestic violence 33

Chapter Six: What to Do When Domestic Violence is Disclosed in Premarital Counseling 45

Chapter Seven: Keeping the Door Open: Ongoing Strategies for Couples, Churches and Pastors 57

Notes 61

Selected Resources 65

Handouts for Use in Premarital Counseling 71
    1. Covenant Circles of Support. 72
    2. Covenantal Communications 74
    3. What Every Couple Needs to Know 76

 4. Power and Control Wheel 78

 5. Equality Wheel. 80

 6. What Ties or Severs the Covenant 82

 7. Contrasting Contractual and Covenantal Relationships 84

 8. Constructive and Destructive Ways of Dealing
  with Anger 86

 9. What Does a Trusting Relationship Look Like? 88

Appendices 91

 1. "Saving the Family: When is Covenant Broken?"
  by Mitzi N. Eilts. 93

 2. Additional Statistics On Domestic Violence 101

 3. Predictors of Domestic Violence. 103

 4. Indicators that a Man May Kill His Partner 105

 5. Accountability 107

 6. Resources Commonly Used in Premarital Counseling 109

 7. "Counseling the Clergy on How to Help Victims of
  Domestic Violence" by SaraKay Smullens. 115

 8. Responding to Domestic Violence:
  Guidelines for Clergy 119

 9. A Community Checklist for Religious Communities 123

About the Writers 125

ACKNOWLEDGMENTS

Many companions walked with me during this writing project – with spirit and skill. If this book is at all useful, inspiring or informative, it is because of our joined venture. I am grateful for those – named and unnamed here – whose music, poetry, books, biblical studies, theological reflections, insightful questions, candid feedback, stories, humor, wisdom, pastoral presence and love shaped my own journey over the years and opened my heart and mind to God's gift of covenantal relationships.

To many persons who have shared stories of pain and courage, joy and wonder, broken covenants and new life with me through the years, thanks for your truth telling.

To staff members of FaithTrust Institute (formerly Center for the Prevention of Sexual and Domestic Violence) who brought the topic of domestic violence to the attention of the Church almost thirty years ago, and especially for the vision of Rev. Dr. Marie M. Fortune, my thanks on behalf of many.

To many clergy colleagues, lay persons, seminary professors, agency staff members, therapists, friends and family members with whom I explored the topics found in this book over the years, thanks for sharing your knowledge and your experiences. I carry special gratitude for the staff and programs of the Samaritan Center of Puget Sound (formerly Presbyterian Counseling Service) in Seattle, Washington; you have enriched my ministry for over twenty years.

To those who provided practical support at crucial junctures – the King County Library System, Seattle Public Library, computer consultants, and assorted others – my respectful thanks.

To Carol Adams, Rev. Thelma B. Burgonio-Watson, Rev. Luis Carriere, Dr. Cher N. Edwards, Dr. Scott Edwards, Rev. Dr. Lucy Forster-Smith, Rev. Dr. Marie M. Fortune, Rev. Dr. David Kratz, Rev. Aleese Moore-Orbih, Dr. James Newton Poling – all of whom read portions or all of the manuscript at various stages along the way – my thanks for suggestions which significantly enriched the final draft. My particular thanks to Dr. Anne Ganley for sharing not only your knowledge of the complex dynamics of domestic violence, but also your outstanding editorial wisdom.

To Jean Anton, a woman of extraordinary commitment to relationships of well-being and integrity, and an editor with remarkable gifts and skills – including patience, computer savvy, empathy, focus, gentle nudging and writing – my thanks for keeping the vision before us and for opening yourself to a collaborative process as this project unfolded.

Susan Yarrow Morris

PREFACE

Dear Colleague…A Letter of Concern and Challenge…

Have you witnessed or participated in a story similar to those described below? (The stories are compiled from real events; names and identifying features have been changed to protect the individuals.)

> When meeting with their pastor in preparation for their wedding service, Mary and Jeff both acknowledged, "We fight a lot, but we usually work it out." The pastor responded, "That's the important thing. Every couple has conflicts, but when partners can work through them and stay together, that's a sign of a healthy relationship." At the next premarital counseling session, Mary cautiously asked the pastor, "What if we fight and don't work it out?" The pastor replied, "When that happens, we suggest that you try to be more loving to each other, and that you pray for God's help." No more was said, and the wedding took place. Two years later, after the birth of their baby, Mary turned up at a battered women's shelter, describing a long nightmare of domestic violence, both before and after the wedding.

> Lorraine, who had grown up in the church and whose parents were considered "pillars of the church," asked her pastor to officiate at her wedding. During the first two premarital counseling sessions, the pastor noticed some disturbing signs and was concerned about the possibility of, or potential for, domestic violence in the relationship. Brian never let Lorraine speak for herself; he answered questions for her. If she attempted to answer the questions herself, he often stared at her in an intimidating manner. The pastor had an unsettling feeling that Lorraine was afraid of Brian. As was her custom, the pastor met for a third session with the couple. During this session, among other topics, she shared information and resources related to domestic violence, privately hoping Lorraine would call the local shelter and get some support for calling off the wedding. This did not happen and they met for the fourth premarital counseling session. The dynamics between

Lorraine and Brian seemed more troubling than ever, and it became clear to the pastor that she could not, in good faith, officiate at the wedding.

The whole family was upset with their beloved family pastor, who could not share her reasons with them because of her commitment to confidentiality. They found another pastor to officiate at their wedding, and headed off to Europe where Brian served in the military. Six months later, Lorraine returned home and filed for divorce, after having been beaten so badly that she had required hospitalization. After a time, the family talked with their pastor, saying, "We made a mistake. We're sorry." The pastor regretted the tragedy of this couple's story and pledged to learn more effective ways to address domestic violence in her premarital counseling.

———

Rich is a friend and pastoral colleague. He has served several churches over the past twenty years in three different locations in the U.S. and is a highly respected preacher, pastor and teacher. We have shared lectionary study, parish concerns, and theological dialogues, as well as offering mutual support for our personal journeys in ministry over several years. Recently, we explored the topic of premarital counseling – what each of us includes, which resources we find helpful, and how we view this in the larger context of our ministries. At one point I asked him how he addresses domestic violence in his premarital counseling. I was surprised by his response: "Oh, I just don't go there. I'd rather not open that door – it's way too complicated." Since that conversation, I've found that Rich is not alone. Many other fine pastors have shared their hesitancy about opening this door in their premarital counseling.

———

"I'd rather not open that door…"

As a pastor who tries to respond faithfully when I sense God is calling me to open doors to new life, liberation and hope in this sacred vocation of ordained ministry, I find there is a part of me, too, that would prefer not to open the door that addresses domestic violence. I wish there were not the need to do so. I wish that our cultural reality were a less violent, more respectful context in which to live and love. I wish that there were more of a "guarantee" that if I followed some easy steps in my pastoral counseling, the scenarios would turn out differently from those recounted above.

For a few years early in my ministry, I avoided the topic of domestic violence,

PREFACE

despite the information I was hearing and reading from others. It had not been a reality in my own life journey, and I clung to the naïve hope that such horrors occurred rarely and only to a particular kind of person. Surely "that kind of person" would not be in the community of faith *I* was serving. In addition, I lacked confidence that I would know what to do or say that would actually *help* intimate partners and couples. I feared that I might make things worse, rather than better.

My own heart, mind, and ministry were profoundly transformed when, in my work as a campus minister, I encountered several courageous women whose lives had been ravaged by the experience of domestic violence. These women came to me seeking a listening ear, an acknowledgement of their true and painful stories, and some resources of our shared faith that might offer a sense of God's presence in the midst of their lives. As I listened to each of these women, different stories unfolded, but the impact of the violation each had experienced was real. I finally began to "get it." As a pastor, never again could I intentionally keep that door closed.

I knew that, from that point forward, I would have to open the door, rather than shut out the opportunity to help victims find healing and help abusers find support to change. I committed myself to learning all that I could about domestic violence and to naming it as a reality in my preaching and teaching and, particularly, in designing and directing marriage preparation ministries in campus ministry and in two parishes. I also realized the importance of committing myself, in all that I do, to providing encouragement for relationships of mutuality, justice, respect and covenant love in the context of the Christian faith.

Here I am, thirty years later, surely the wiser, and yet far from being an expert about violence in intimate relationships, though the painful stories have been shared not only in my pastoral work but, sadly, in my own extended family circle as well. Stories like those at the beginning of this book have been shared with me by colleagues who felt they had done their pastoral best to deal with domestic violence in their encounters with couples, but who were concerned that their efforts were neither adequate nor effective. Much has changed over these years. Pastors no longer need to be the experts or feel that we must "fix" tragic situations alone. We are now blessed with community resources that are informative, inspiring and essential as we do our various ministries with individuals, couples and families of all kinds. This is good news for all of us, but, most importantly, for those persons whom we serve in this sacred pastoral relationship.

As challenging as it may be, it behooves us to open the door to the topic of domestic violence as a part of our premarital counseling because it is a part of the truth telling we're called to do as ministers of the Gospel and because it is central to the pastoral task of offering hope and renewed life. That is what this resource is all about. The images of covenant love offered from the prophet Hosea have been central to my work in these ministries.

> On that day, says the Lord, you will call me, "My husband," and no longer will you call me, 'My Baal.'…I will make for you a covenant on that day with the wild animals, the birds of the air, and the creeping things of the ground; and I will abolish the bow, the sword, and war from the land; and I will make you lie down in safety. And I will take you for my wife forever; I will take you for my wife in righteousness and in justice, in steadfast love, and in mercy. I will take you for my wife in faithfulness…
>
> (Hosea 2:16-20, excerpts)[1]

This book is written, then, from my experience as a pastor and from my sense of urgency as a colleague who reads the newspaper stories day after day and who knows that marriage is not only a holy calling but also represents one of the most common interpersonal contexts in which aggression toward women occurs. Most of all, it is based on my belief that, together, we can be a part of creating a "new heaven and a new earth" (Revelation 21:1) in which relationships can thrive and persons can live "abundantly" (John 10:10).

CHAPTER ONE

INTRODUCTION:
BEGINNING WITH US, THE PASTORS

Pastoral premarital counseling takes place in a theological, cultural and personal context, which is different for each of us. When we are at our best as ministers, we work and pray for congruency between what we believe (our faith lives) and what we do (our ministry lives). Premarital counseling is part of our pastoral work of teaching, preaching and empowering others to live Jesus' Gospel of love and justice and mutuality. Rather than being an activity we do apart from the "more important" aspects of our ministry, it is, in fact, central to our ministry.

Many of us feel overwhelmed by tasks and meetings related to keeping our churches thriving or even surviving in these days of institutional challenges. If we do our work in settings such as colleges or hospitals, administrative demands can take our best attention and time. As we prioritize our time and efforts, premarital counseling may not seem to rise to the top of our "to do" lists. Some colleagues have candidly described "irritation" at the time and effort required by premarital counseling when other tasks seem more important. Others have expressed a lack of competence or even interest in this aspect of ministry. For these and many other reasons, it appears that for many pastors, premarital counseling itself is a challenge.

Because this is a reality for many of us, the suggestion that we need to address domestic violence within premarital counseling may compound the challenge. Thus it is essential to begin with candid reflections related to our personal and theological foundations. When we do, we may find we are (for good reasons) resistant to opening the door to dealing with the topic of domestic violence in the context of pastoral premarital counseling. The complex challenges of domestic violence may seem daunting and dangerous, so we may choose not to address them at all. Some of us have been profoundly shaped by a theology of suffering and/or a culture of strict gender roles which make it difficult for us to ask critical questions or to embrace a covenant theology of liberation, mutuality and justice. We may believe that the issue of domestic violence is "overblown" and that it is unlikely to occur within the congregations or other settings in

CHAPTER ONE

which we serve. Some of us may have had our own personal encounters with the topic, suggesting that lingering confusion or unfinished healing prevents us from knowing how to proceed. Many feel we are doing the best we can, and we hold out the hope that this topic will not need to be addressed in our pastoral settings. However, as experts in the field have suggested, sometimes thoughtful but ill-informed actions may do more harm than good when dealing with domestic violence.

Acknowledging our own starting place with regard to domestic violence, and our beliefs and practices related to premarital counseling, is a significant first step in opening a door that tends to stay tightly closed. The next step is exploring the many reasons why we *must* address domestic violence in our premarital counseling. These include the following.

Many of our efforts in ministry have to do with supporting and encouraging faith-filled covenantal relationships. Our preaching focuses on the Good News as it inspires daily lives and relationships, continually calling forth a faithful response to God's gift of love. Much of our pastoral work and educational efforts– including premarital counseling – involves interpreting the Gospel and empowering our parishioners to live in loving relationships of respect and equality.

As we know, domestic violence rips apart the very fabric of the covenantal relationships we work so diligently to sustain. Any form of domestic violence damages the foundation of mutual trust, which is essential in a covenantal relationship. Furthermore, domestic violence impacts not only individuals and relationships but communities of faith and friendship as well. Because of its prevalence and the devastating extent of its impact on families and communities, it is our obligation to do everything we can to end domestic violence.

Because we know that "almost all (domestic) violence occurs either before the marriage itself or before the birth of the first child,"[2] premarital counseling offers a unique context in which to screen for existing abuse and to educate for prevention of future abuse. Good pastoral premarital counseling will help couples look honestly at the dynamics of their interactions, offer information and strategies that will empower the best of covenantal life, and screen individual partners for past or present patterns of violence.

CHAPTER ONE

This door cannot be opened unless we are prepared to do our own honest work, both personally and theologically. As a beginning place, I would suggest that we need to have a *commitment to:*

- Ongoing biblical and theological reflection related to covenantal relationships, and to developing ministries of education and nurture for them.

- Personal education, therapy (if appropriate) and training about domestic violence.

- Basic guidelines and ethics for doing couples' counseling.

- Preparation of resources and handouts for engaged couples that include theological affirmations and domestic violence information.

- Keeping as our priority the safety of persons at risk above all else.

We need to have done our homework, attended training on domestic violence, and have a *working familiarity with:*

- Definitions of domestic violence and implications for family life.

- Basic statistics related to domestic violence.

- Local resources – shelters, counselors, programs for victims and abusers.

- Faith dimensions of domestic violence for victims and abusers.

- Effective tools and strategies for addressing domestic violence with couples and for screening of individual partners.

- Pastoral or counseling colleagues with whom we can share resources, wisdom, and information.

This basic guidebook is intended to assist us to be prepared – spiritually, personally, intellectually and pastorally – to address domestic violence in premarital counseling. I hope that it enables us to open the door with greater confidence and conviction, as well as improved competence.

CHAPTER TWO
A BIBLICAL AND THEOLOGICAL FOUNDATION FOR PREMARITAL COUNSELING THAT ADDRESSES DOMESTIC VIOLENCE

Exploring Covenant Theology[3]

Exploring and affirming a theology of covenantal relationships is a way to lay a foundation for ministries of pastoral care and attention to healthy relationships. In situations of domestic violence, the covenant is broken by violence of any kind. By examining a theology of covenantal relationships, we can better understand how best to approach these situations.

Embedded throughout the larger biblical story are found many small covenant stories – stories of covenant making, covenant keeping, covenant renewing and covenant breaking. These stories help us understand God's covenants with humankind and our covenants with one another in God. In the lives of very real human beings, covenant life is experienced, celebrated and renewed – and lamented when broken.

In Genesis, Noah is chosen to participate in the establishment of a covenant for all times between God and God's people. Through the story, we learn that covenantal relationships matter more than any other, that covenantal partners make pledges to pay attention to one another and to remember one another at all times, and that symbols are created that remind partners of their covenants. It is affirmed that in covenantal relationships, faithfulness is the primary activity.

Many Psalms (15, 90, 102, 133, 139 and others) include references to our covenant partner, God/Yahweh, as faithful, the source of inspiration, salvation and protection in the midst of chaos and despair, a compassionate and just Holy One who calls forth similar actions from us. In other biblical texts (Hosea, Jeremiah, Paul's Letters, Hebrews, and more) we are given glimpses of covenantal life in which we are to participate in creating, sustaining and renewing activities.

Throughout the Gospels, Jesus shapes our understanding of covenantal relationships by his teaching and preaching ministry. As he helps others explore who and how God loves covenantally, whether sitting at the feast table with friends or feeding the unknown crowds on a hillside, we are called to do the same. All are welcomed to the table; the least, lost and last of the world are invited into the circle. Power is shared among all the people in a radical new way as God's love is given and received and used to empower and liberate persons for discipleship in the world. All covenant partners – all God's children, all humankind – have an equal voice when this power is shared. Jesus calls us to participate in the transformative work of creating covenantal relationships, which are life-giving not only personally but also in the larger world. When we choose to join another in covenantal love, we are not entertaining a romantic notion, nor are we offering intellectual assent to an idea. We agree to live with one another in a unique reflection of God's remarkable love for humankind. It is the covenant bond – the relationship, the connection – which is to be honored, tended, and respected.

The affirmations that emerge from scripture related to covenantal relationships might be summarized as follows:

Covenantal relationships are:

- Chosen by partners who share a mutual love for one another.
- Sealed by mutual vows or promises.
- Open-ended (not knowing the outcome, trusting the journey together).
- Marked primarily by faithfulness, fidelity to God's intentions for life abundant.
- Intended to be forever, revised and renewed over and over again.
- Life-giving, not only to the partners but to the world about them.
- Ended when the covenant is violated by one or both partners.

In which covenant partners:

- Recreate and renew the covenant at any time.
- Celebrate their covenant by offering symbols and sharing rituals.
- Are held accountable for actions, intentions and words.
- Embody their covenant promises in daily life by speaking the truth in love, listening patiently, working through conflicts with mutual respect.
- Provide for one another a safe, kind and nurturing haven for body, mind

- and spirit.
- Belong to one another without possessing each other.
- Honor God's gift of life and love by living gratefully and thoughtfully.

Affirming a covenant theology as a basis for family and relational ministry opens the door for a wide variety of programmatic and pastoral efforts in local churches or in other settings for ministry. Including a vision of covenant life in sermons and classes; in fellowship gatherings and social justice work; in pastoral counseling, premarital counseling, and educational settings for all ages can help persons of faith become familiar with this very unique reality called "covenant life."

Alongside our work of supporting relationships based on the biblical model of covenant must be the naming of dynamics that prevent such relationships from flourishing and which, ultimately, destroy them. Domestic violence does just that; it damages relationships that were initially founded upon the characteristics listed above. In particular, the last five characteristics, when present in a relationship of love, not only will protect against domestic violence becoming a reality, but are also the most profoundly damaged when domestic violence does occur.

Common Theological Challenges when Exploring the Topic of Covenant with Couples

Inherent in the task of crafting a theology of covenantal relationships are some challenges for the pastor related to the reality of domestic violence.

First, there is the tendency for many pastors to emphasize the "forever/come what may" nature of covenant life without paying equal attention to the other dimensions listed above. When this occurs, "forever" becomes an absolute truth that does not leave any room for questions related to the health and well-being of the relationship or the covenant partners. Thus, we have heard story after story of women who made extraordinary efforts to stay with their partners, even when they were victims of domestic violence, because they believed that marriage "should be forever" or that God would judge them sinners if they left their relationships. One such survivor sought guidance from her pastor after numerous violent incidents. His response: "It is God's will that you stay with your husband and try harder to be a good Christian wife." This misinterpretation of one of the biblical foundations of covenant theology can lead to further abuse and often to a woman's abandonment by her church community at a time when she most needs their support.

A pastor describing covenant life can provide clarity and compassion when s/he helps couples understand that "forever" is not the only goal of a covenantal relationship. "Forever" *joined* with well-being of partners, and bond *joined* with mutual respect, hope, and life shared in the larger community, become the goals of a covenantal relationship. From time to time, then, the relationship needs to be evaluated on the basis of *many* dimensions, which are equally as significant as "forever."

This emphasis on "forever/come what may" also begs the question about how covenants end. If, as has been proposed by some, covenants end when one or both partners violate the bond in some way (e.g., abuse), what happens next? When is righteous rage appropriate? When is forgiveness possible? Can reconciliation ever be a hoped-for outcome?

Mitzi N. Eilts, in an especially helpful article, "Saving the Family: When Is Covenant Broken?" (see complete article in Appendix 1), explores the biblical foundations for covenant life with particular attention to broken and violated trust due to violence and abuse within relationships. Her insights give pastors the language and background necessary to articulate a theology of covenant life that includes not only joyful expectations but also significant obligations. As we prepare to work with engaged couples, it is necessary that we do our own theological reflection on these and related topics. Our work with couples will surely be more authentic and helpful. Once again, we have some excellent resources available for doing this work; many are listed in the Selected Resources and Appendices.

A second challenge in sharing the scriptural and theological basis for covenantal relationships is the idea of "sacrificial love." The thinking goes like this: Because Jesus gave his life in love for God and God's people, the highest good we might do as people of faith is to give our lives in love. Although this may be a theological truth in general, sadly, many women take on this role in marriages in which violence and abuse are present. They sacrifice their own sacred selves in submission to a partner's control and dominance. They sacrifice hopes and dreams and the ability to have their own voices to the status they believe marriage offers. A pastor can help a couple understand that true covenant love calls us not to negation of self but to mutual empowerment of selves, and that the gift of Jesus' life in love is that others might thrive and live.

A third challenge emerges when Scriptural passages are misused to justify control, domination, or abuse within a relationship.

CHAPTER TWO

> Wives, be subject to your husbands as you are to the Lord.
> For the husband is the head of the wife just as Christ is the
> head of the church, the body of which he is the Savior.
>
> (Ephesians 5:22-23)

This passage has at times been misinterpreted to justify submission of wives to their husbands. A true interpretation, however, is very different.

> This means that there are times in a Christian marriage when a wife should give way to her husband and recognize his interests as well as her own. But the husband's headship suggested here does not mean a role of unquestioned authority to which you are to be blindly obedient. What is described here is a model based on Christ's relationship to the church: Jesus was the servant of all who followed him and he gave himself up for them. Never did he order people around, threaten, hit, or frighten them.
>
> Almost all the rest of this passage from Ephesians spells out the instructions to the husband in his treatment of his wife: he is to be to her as Christ was to the church. This means he is to serve her needs and be willing to sacrifice himself for her if need be…He is to love his wife as himself, to nourish and cherish her.
>
> – Rev. Dr. Marie M. Fortune[4]

Reading this passage through the lens of covenant affirms that the primary message is this: "Be subject to one another out of reverence for Christ." This reflects mutuality, reverence and equality shared in a relationship that dwells in the love and mercy of Christ, a covenantal relationship.

Although there are many other theological challenges related to biblical exploration of covenant in light of the reality of domestic violence, in my experience with couples and with victims of domestic violence, these three are especially common. Our work is to come to a place of peace with our own affirmations, as well as to acknowledge the ongoing challenges, as we do this important work with couples.

In the following chapters, you will find specific suggestions about how we can move from a foundation of joyful, hope-filled covenant love to include issues of domestic violence in our premarital counseling.

As I have reflected on this rich and lively dynamic of covenant as the biblical and theological heartbeat of my own ministry, I am aware that the gift of human love holds great mystery such that all the books in the world cannot fully describe. And so I have also been inspired by art, music, poetry, literature, theater, etc. I include here several poems that offer other images for covenantal relationships, for use with couples in premarital and other counseling situations. They give us images of safety, equality, mutuality, respect and trust – all dimensions of life-giving covenantal relationships in which there is no space for partner violence or abuse. I also invite you to draw courage in this task from your own sources of inspiration for your pastoral work.

A Third Body

A man and a woman sit near each other, and they do not long
at this moment to be older, or younger, nor born
in any other nation, or time, or place.
They are content to be where they are, talking or not-talking.
Their breaths together feed someone whom we do not know.
The man sees the way his fingers move;
he sees her hands close around a book she hands to him.
They obey a third body that they share in common.
They have made a promise to love that body.
Age may come, parting may come, death will come.
A man and a woman sit near each other;
as they breathe they feed someone we do not know,
someone we know of, whom we have never seen.

– Robert Bly[5]

CHAPTER TWO

Beyond What

We reach for destinies beyond
what we have come to know
and in the romantic hush
of promises
perceive each
the other's life
as known mystery.
Shared. But inviolate.
No melting. No squeezing
into One.
We swing our eyes around
as well as side to side
to see the world.

To choose, renounce,
this, or that —
call it a council between equals
call it love.

— Alice Walker [6]

The Conditions

Don't ask a vow of obedience,
Or try to do my thinking for me.
In this century the cause has been
That I might greet you as an equal.
Ask, instead, if I will sleep
In the crook of your arm,
Spend free hours with you,
Carry children (yours and mine)
Beneath my heart.
Then, perhaps, we can learn
If there are strong things masculine
And sweet things feminine
For which no battle need be fought.

— Bennie Lee Sinclair [7]

CHAPTER THREE
WHAT EVERY PASTOR NEEDS TO KNOW ABOUT DOMESTIC VIOLENCE

As we prepare to address domestic violence in premarital counseling, we draw upon our own personal and pastoral experiences related to the topic. In addition, we need to learn as much as we can about the topic from those who do research and work with both perpetrators and survivors of domestic violence. In this chapter, I have distilled the essential aspects of domestic violence – definitions, statistics, basic information. Much more is available on websites, in books and articles, and in training programs. See the Selected Resources at the end of this book for more information.

As I read this and other related information, I am continually aware that domestic violence is not just "an issue" for discussion, but reflects a major social and moral dimension of our culture. As I consider the faces behind the statistics and the relationships reflected in the definitions, I realize that we are called to provide a faithful and serious response in our various settings for ministry.

What is Domestic Violence?[8]

Domestic violence is a pattern of behavior used by one partner in an intimate relationship to establish power and control over another person through fear and intimidation, often including the use of or threat of violence. Domestic violence happens when one person believes he or she is entitled to control another. Victims can be of any age, race, gender, sexual orientation, religion, or socioeconomic level. Assault, battering and domestic violence are crimes.

Abuse of an intimate partner can take many forms. Domestic violence may include physical abuse, sexual abuse, emotional abuse, economic abuse, using children, threats, using male privilege, intimidation, isolation, and a variety of other tactics used to maintain fear, intimidation and power. In all cultures, the abusers are most commonly the men of the family. Women are most commonly the victims of violence, although men may also be victims. Because the huge majority of domestic violence is perpetrated by men against women, we will use the pronoun "she" to refer to victims/survivors and "he" to refer to abusers. The tactics used by abusers to maintain power and control generally fall into one or more of the following categories:

- Physical Abuse – Physical abuse can include a wide range of behaviors, such as pushing, hitting, shoving, grabbing, slapping, kicking, restraining, and punching. More extreme cases of physical abuse may include the use of weapons, strangling, and murder. Physical violence often begins with what is excused as trivial contacts, which then escalate into more frequent and more serious attacks.

- Sexual Abuse – Includes any sexual activity that is forced on, or unwanted and declined by, the partner. A physical attack by the abuser may be accompanied by sexual violence wherein the woman is forced to have sexual intercourse with her abuser.

- Psychological Abuse – Psychological or emotional abuse can include constant verbal abuse (e.g., name-calling or putdowns), harassment, excessive possessiveness, stalking, isolating the victim from friends and family, deprivation of physical and economic resources, attacks against property or pets, and suicidal behavior or threats.

Domestic violence tends to escalate in severity and frequency over time. It often begins with behaviors such as threats, name calling, violence in the presence of the victim (e.g., punching a fist through a wall), and/or damage to objects or pets. It may escalate to restraining, pushing, slapping, and/or pinching. The battering may include punching, kicking, biting, sexual assault, tripping, or throwing. It may become life-threatening with serious behaviors such as choking, breaking bones, or the use of weapons.

Reviewing some significant statistics can be enlightening for us. From the National Center for Injury Prevention and Control:[9]

- Nearly 5.3 million intimate partner victimizations occur each year among U.S. women ages 18 and older. This violence results in nearly 2 million injuries and nearly 1,300 deaths.

- Intimate partner violence occurs across all populations, irrespective of social, economic, religious, or cultural group. However, young women and those below the poverty line are disproportionately affected.

- Nearly 25% of women have been raped and/or physically assaulted by an intimate partner at some point in their lives, and more than 40% of

CHAPTER THREE

the women who experience partner rapes and physical assaults sustain a physical injury.

- As many as 324,000 women each year experience intimate partner violence during their pregnancies.

Important Facts about Domestic Violence[10]

Fact No. 1: Domestic violence is a systematic pattern of abusive behavior that develops and escalates over time.

Domestic violence and abuse is *not* about sudden loss of control. It does not "erupt" suddenly from out of nowhere. On the contrary, it is a systematic pattern of behavior used to control a loved one. Sometimes violence grows out of immediate anger, but in many other instances, batterers are very calm and intentional about their abuse. Often, what may have begun as a subtle form of abuse grows over a period of time into more overt violence. Left unchecked, frequency and intensity can escalate, even to the point of ending in murder and/or suicide. *Domestic violence is a systematic pattern of abusive behavior that develops and escalates over time.*

Fact No. 2: Women do not provoke violence in an intimate relationship.

Another false assumption is that battered women provoke their abuse. The abuser bears sole responsibility for his actions. There is no behavior on the part of the victim that causes or excuses abuse. Offenders often attempt to falsely accuse and disgrace their victims in order to shift blame away from themselves. It is important to remember that, even in those cases where the victim has violated the marriage in some way, violence is never a legitimate response. The abuser has other avenues of appropriate response available – to seek outside help, or to leave the situation. Violence is never an appropriate response. *Women do not provoke the violence.*

Fact No. 3: The desire for power and control over others, not alcohol or drug use, is the root cause of domestic violence.

It is a popular misconception that alcohol and drug use "causes" domestic violence, and that the elimination of the substance abuse problem will eliminate the problem of violence. While it is true that drug and alcohol use often co-occurs with domestic violence, many studies have revealed that alcohol and drugs do not cause violence in the home. Clearly the frequency of violent incidents and severity of injury may be increased under the influence, but neither alcohol nor drugs is at the root of the violence. Rather, the desire for power and control over another person is at the root of the violence. Not all batterers drink or abuse drugs, nor do all those who drink or abuse drugs batter. When substance abuse and violence co-occur, each must be addressed separately. *The desire for power and control over others, not alcohol or drug use, is the root cause of domestic violence.*

Fact No. 4: Domestic violence and abuse can take many different forms, all of which can destroy a person's well-being.

Usually we think of domestic violence in terms of physical or sexual abuse. But abuse takes many forms. Most clearly defined are physical, verbal, sexual, spiritual, emotional, economic, social, and psychological abuse. These frequently coexist and produce a pattern of relationship in which the abuser's behavior intimidates the victim and cuts her off from healthy relationships in family, church, and workplace; robs her of the financial independence to change her circumstances; saps her sense of self-worth and self-determination; and leaves her in constant fear for her safety and that of her children. Many victims of domestic violence become so isolated and ashamed that they begin to believe that *they* are the problem, somehow deserving the abuse they receive. They become desensitized to their emotions and hopeless for change. *Violence and abuse take many forms and can be measured by their destructive effects on the well-being of the victim.*

Fact No. 5: It is possible for abusive men to change only after acknowledgement of their problem and a commitment to hard work over a period of time.

Certainly abusive men can change. God changes hearts. But, changed behavior does not occur overnight or simply because one is sorry. Change begins with surrender. The abuser must admit that he has a problem. Unfortunately, many abusers are unwilling to admit this. These men remain dangerous and will not change as long as they refuse to take responsibility for their behavior. Those who acknowledge their problem and seek help must demonstrate a commitment to be accountable. *Abusive men can change. Real change requires time and hard work.*

CHAPTER THREE

Common Questions about Domestic Violence[11]

How do I know if someone is a victim of domestic violence?

There is no simple way to tell is someone is a victim of domestic violence. Women who are being battered are as different from one other as are non-battered women. They come from all walks of life, all races, all educational backgrounds, and all religions. A battered woman might be the Vice-President of your local bank, your child's Sunday school teacher, your beautician or your dentist. Anyone experiencing any of the patterns of abuse (physical, sexual, psychological, or attacks against property and pets) is a victim of domestic violence.

Who are batterers?

Just as with battered women, men who batter fall into no specific categories. They also come from all class backgrounds, races, religions, and walks of life. They may be unemployed or highly-paid professionals. The batterer may be a good provider, a sober and upstanding member of the community, and a respected member of his congregation.

Why does she stay?[12]

The reasons why women stay in abusive relationships are complicated and vary with each individual. Often they are a combination of the following:

The batterer's escalating controlling behaviors – Victims always have to consult their knowledge of what abusers are likely to do if they leave, seek help, or take suggestions from caring professionals or concerned friends. Sometimes it is safer for them and their children *not* to leave, or to get a protection order, or to tell their minister everything.

Fear – Abused women and their children are in the most danger of being battered when they try to leave or attempt to end the relationship.

"For the children" – Sometimes women remain in abusive relationships because they feel even an abusive father is better than no father at all, or they fear that they may not have the strength to live alone and care for their children. They may also be anxious about the custody process, finances, or the possibility of

losing their children. Abusers often threaten to hurt the children or to attempt to gain sole custody.

Lack of Economic Resources – Many abused women feel they will not be able to sustain an adequate life for themselves and their children and are concerned about the repercussions, both financial and emotional, of going through a divorce process.

Isolation – Abusers often try to keep the victim isolated from her usual network of support and care, so at a time when she may most need the support, she is prevented from accessing it.

Societal Denial – Abusers are often appealing, popular, and professionally competent, treating those in their community and work lives very differently from those with whom they live. Women often stay in abusive relationships because they fear, with good reason, that no one will believe their experiences.

Religious and Cultural Pressures – Many women believe it is their religious duty to stay in a covenantal relationship "until death us do part." Some fear their communities of faith may not welcome them if they separate or divorce.

Commitment to the Partner and Hope for Change – Often abused women try to honor the commitment of their marriage vows, hoping that, in time, with love, the abuse will stop. Research indicates that domestic violence does not stop without intervention from professionals trained in this area, and a recognition by the abuser that the abusive behavior is his responsibility. Abusers often promise that "it will never happen again," and their partners cling to that hope. Without intervention, however, the abuser will continue to abuse.

Belief in Counseling for the Abuser – Women sometimes believe couples' counseling will change their partners and they will stop the abuse. Experience informs us that attending counseling or therapy sessions will not help. For abusers to change, they must become deeply and authentically involved in the process by facing their problems, ceasing to blame others and ending all abusive behaviors. This happens most effectively in a long term batterers' intervention program involving the abusive partner without the victim.

The Immobilizing Impact of Shame and Humiliation – Abused women suffer from many emotional and psychological traumas, such as shame and humiliation, which can keep them from taking action leading to health and healing.

The Process of Leaving Issues – Most abused women leave and return several times before permanently separating from their abusers, due to some of the above reasons. The process may take a long time, as the woman begins to feel increasingly confident of resources and of her own strength to survive alone. Because of the possible danger involved in separation, it is essential that an abused woman leave in the safest way possible, with knowledge of the available resources and a plan for their use.

The Impact of Domestic Violence

> The societal costs of domestic violence are staggering to our educational systems, our legal systems, our health systems, our criminal justice systems, our neighborhoods, our workplaces, and our congregations.
>
> Particularly vulnerable are the future generations. Children who witness abuse have ringside seats. Even when they are not directly abused themselves, they are six times more likely to commit suicide, 24 times more likely to commit a sexual assault, 50% more likely to abuse drugs and alcohol, and 74% more likely to commit crimes against others. Clearly the violence that these children witness radiates outward to society, and down through the generations.
>
> – Nancy Murphy [13]

Given the statistics on the pervasiveness of domestic violence, together with a picture of its devastating impact on our congregations and communities, it becomes clear why it is critical that we make use of the opportunity presented to us in premarital counseling to address abuse and to look for ways to promote peaceful family relationships and prevent further violence.

Opening the door to addressing domestic violence in premarital counseling looks more doable as we reflect on our own personal and faith journeys, do some biblical and theological groundwork, and acquaint ourselves with basic information about domestic violence. We now turn to the components of our premarital counseling practices, with a particular eye to the inclusion of domestic violence.

CHAPTER FOUR
COMPONENTS OF PASTORAL PREMARITAL COUNSELING

Several variables come into play as we design premarital counseling programs in our particular pastoral settings. These are especially relevant to our task at hand – addressing the issue of domestic violence in premarital counseling.

Goals

Historically, the goal of premarital counseling has focused on planning the wedding service, with special attention to interpreting denominational liturgical rituals and faith traditions. Pastors have also used this time to reflect theologically and biblically with couples on the meaning of marriage and covenant promises. As we work with couples who have made a decision to marry, we have welcomed the opportunity for thoughtful reflection focused on a hopeful, joyful shared future. It can be one of our more delightful pastoral encounters, as we meet with couples who are eagerly planning a significant, life-changing event.

Given the current statistics related to domestic violence and divorce, I believe we need to be prepared to do *more* in premarital counseling than simply "plan the wedding." If we are to take our responsibility seriously as we are given this unique opportunity to meet with couples at a significant juncture in their lives, it is also important that we do the following:

- Provide a setting for candid conversations between partners related to topics relevant to covenant life – communication, family histories, values and beliefs, differences and similarities, ethnic traditions, faith dimensions, work and play, sexuality and intimacy, role expectations, extended family issues, money, vocations, etc.

- Educate couples together about the components of thriving, life-giving, faithful covenant partnerships and the skills necessary to sustain such relationships.

- In individual sessions with each of the partners early in the premarital counseling process, assess the health and potential for health in the relationship, including screening for past, current or possible future domestic violence.

- Educate couples together about domestic violence as an unacceptable component of covenantal relationships, defining various types of violence and providing current statistics, warning signs, and information about community programs that offer help for victims and abusers.

- If, as a result of questions asked in individual screening sessions or behavior observed in couples' sessions, domestic violence is either explicitly disclosed by one or both partners or is suspected by the pastor, respond appropriately, keeping the safety of the victim the highest priority.

These goals assume that we know something about these topics, and that we'll have the time and resources needed to do the job. None of us will meet these goals perfectly with every couple, and some of us may resist adding such tasks, given realistic limits on our time and energy.

However, good intentions and brief seminary courses taken years ago are no longer enough to do this work. We need to respond to the reality of domestic violence, which occurs in families from all religious traditions – even families in our own faith communities – by offering premarital counseling that includes these additional goals. And we need to seek the training and do the reading that will enable us to be knowledgeable and effective in this task.

Resources abound to prepare us to meet these goals. (See the Selected Resources and Appendices.) The next chapter describes strategies for addressing domestic violence within premarital counseling.

If we believe that these goals are important and that we are *not* able to fulfill them by ourselves, we can creatively work with other professionals in our communities to see that they are met. These goals assume that our work with engaged couples is more than perfunctory; it is essential in doing preventive and proactive work with them. These goals are the fundamental element that sets the tone for what we include and how we proceed in our premarital counseling.

Context

As is always the case in our premarital counseling, questions or exercises for couples must honor the unique situational, racial/ethnic and cultural context of each partner. Learning about cultural traditions and customs is part of the preparation we must do in this sacred work. Because I have worked with couples from a wonderful variety of racial/ethnic and faith traditions over the years, I have learned how important it is for us to study topics such as courtship and dowry customs, communication patterns, attitudes toward domestic violence, symbols and meanings of language within a particular context. Not doing so may lead to a perception of unintended disrespect and unhelpful conversations at the least, or, more seriously, to escalation of the potential for domestic violence.

For example, as a Caucasian woman, I recognize that my knowledge and experience of other cultures is limited. When I was asked to officiate at the wedding services of several couples in the Filipino community, it was very helpful that I met with a Filipino pastor and several members of the Filipino community. They shared with me some of the important dimensions of Filipino relational life (gender dynamics, language meanings, traditions and customs) and of the wedding service itself (rituals, traditions, assumptions). The couples with whom I worked appreciated my efforts to understand their cultural norms while we worked together to explore covenant theology and related topics in the planning of their wedding services.

Because domestic violence affects people regardless of race, ethnicity, class, sexual or gender identity, religious affiliation, age, immigration status or ability, we will want to communicate our respect for all persons, not only in our conversations but also in any written materials used for premarital counseling or wedding service planning. Refining exercises, questions, and conversation topics to match the realities of each couple is important, related not only to racial/ethnic and cultural background, but to family constellation as well. Both the process and the content of our premarital counseling should have integrity for couples in which partners are marrying for the second or third (or more) time, and/or in which children are involved. Such information may have an enormous impact as domestic violence is addressed with couples and with individual partners.

Setting

Although most premarital counseling continues to be done within a parish setting, an increasing number of couples are turning to pastors whom they know and trust, who may minister in diverse settings, to officiate at their weddings. Among these are specially trained chaplains – in colleges, hospitals, retirement homes, and other settings. Pastors are also called into private practice, agencies or churches as spiritual directors, pastoral counselors, vocational counselors, campus ministers, writers or educators. Although the goals for our premarital counseling remain the same, the setting in which we do our pastoral work may shape its format and content.

For example, a college chaplain colleague describes as part of her task when working with engaged couples, "trying to make a bridge between the religious dimensions of their college experience and participation in the life of a church when they are settled in a community." It will be important to make the resources in this guide applicable and useful in your particular pastoral setting.

The setting also matters when it comes to the particular policies related to wedding services. In some local churches, for example, it is the policy that wedding services not be conducted for non-members. Other churches look upon non-member weddings as an opportunity for evangelism and hospitality. Most local churches have requirements related to wedding services, including asking the couple to participate in premarital counseling of some sort. Policies related to "off-the-street" or "walk-in" weddings vary from denomination to denomination and often from church to church. This guidebook is based on the premise that premarital counseling should be required prior to the wedding service in all ministry settings for *all* couples.

Regardless of the setting in which our premarital counseling takes place, it is wise, as a reminder of the professional nature of the relationship, to meet in the pastor's study or in another meeting room in the church or workplace. Basic guidelines for professional counseling are recommended wherever we meet couples in this sacred relationship.

Time/Format

As pastors, we tend to design premarital counseling to match our schedules and to a lesser extent, unfortunately, our goals. Most of us find that three or four sessions provide adequate time to touch upon some of the salient topics (including domestic violence), design the wedding service, and provide resources and encouragement for further relationship work. As we take the task more seriously, some pastors are committing to more extensive premarital counseling, ranging from four to six sessions, including homework assignments, the use of assessment instruments, and separate sessions with each of the partners.

Although we most often choose to meet with engaged couples one-on-one, (either by choice or necessity), many clergy are finding that a combination of pastoral counseling and the use of an inventory and/or a session with a skilled therapist can also be an effective partnership. In the latter case, it is important to remember that *neither* the use of an assessment instrument *nor* focused work

CHAPTER FOUR

with a therapist should replace the unique pastoral conversation with individual partners of a couple. It is in this context that relational histories and screening for the potential for domestic violence can most appropriately take place.

Sometimes a church, a consortium of churches, or a local counseling agency offers a group-based program of marriage preparation to which pastors refer couples for attention to relevant topics. The pastor may then meet with couples for one or two sessions to reflect on the workshop experience and to design the wedding service. In some cases, pastors contract with counselors, social workers, therapists or other professionals to do part of the premarital work with couples and then utilize one or two sessions to plan the wedding service. Other formats, using community or church resources (some of which are found in this guide) – such as connecting seasoned married couples in a church as mentors to engaged couples – may affect the format and content of our pastoral work with the couple. We need to be flexible and creative in staying faithful to our task as we invite other supportive resources into the process.

If our pastoral premarital counseling takes place in addition to a couple's participation in a workshop, class or session with a counselor, it is important to know what topics were covered in the class. Follow up these experiences with appropriate questions of couples such as:

- What were three important things you learned about yourselves in the workshop?
- What was the most surprising learning? The most challenging insight?
- What do you celebrate about your covenant?
- How will you keep your covenant mutually life-giving for both of you? What dimensions of your life together will need your special attention?

This conversation, along with our specific focus on covenant life and education about domestic violence, is intended to provide couples with a safe setting for sharing both joys and anxieties about their relationships.

If pastoral premarital counseling takes place in addition to the use of a Premarital Assessment Questionnaire (PAQ) by a trained professional, it will be necessary to know what topics are covered by the instrument and to discuss with the counselor how the results will be shared with the couple and with us. If domestic violence is suspected or revealed in the PAQ, the professional who administered the instrument is, ideally, trained to respond to the situation and to advise appropriate actions. If the pastor is left to share this information with the couple, it will be important to use the guidelines for doing so which follow in Chapter Six.

Given the current information we have about the prevalence and origins of domestic violence, the most effective premarital counseling offered in faith communities should include:

- Focused conversation and education on relevant topics (including domestic violence) *with the couple*.
- Separate sessions *with each partner individually* to screen for domestic violence.
- Appropriate response if domestic violence is disclosed or suspected.
- Wedding service planning *with the couple* together.

In addition, it may be helpful to utilize the services of a trained professional to administer and interpret one of many premarital assessment instruments available, using this information (if permission is given to share) to expand the general topics covered in pastoral counseling. In such cases, shared information can raise our awareness of history or potential for domestic violence within a couple, but it should not replace the individual screening session with the pastor.

Criteria for Selecting Resources to be Used in Conjunction with Pastoral Premarital Counseling

Whether exploring a local premarital workshop program, a nationally produced and directed program, a professional counselor, or a publication, the following questions will help the pastor choose resources which are effective, trustworthy and congruent with the theological and programmatic goals for premarital counseling. We will want to be sure that the resources we use help couples deal with topics honestly and teach ways to sustain mutually life-giving covenantal relationships.

- Is the theology expressed in this resource consistent with the dynamics of biblically-based covenant theology (see Chapter Two)?
- Is this resource used and recommended? By whom? What is the training and experience of those professionals who recommend it?
- Does this resource address domestic violence directly and clearly, protecting the safety of victims above all else?

CHAPTER FOUR

- Is this resource grounded in academic research or other reputable experience?

- Does this resource have a track record of effectiveness for pastors and couples?

- Do we know others we respect who use this resource? Do we know and trust the persons involved (the writers, leaders, therapists, etc.)?

- Is the resource user friendly, interesting, knowledgeable, current, relevant for couples considering covenant life together?

- What is the goal of this resource: To generate couple conversation? To educate with specific tools and strategies? To inspire couples to live together in mutual trust and respect? To cover general topics of premarital interest? To set a beginning tone for couple work together before referring a couple to a skilled therapist? Other?

Because there are many published resources (e.g., Premarital Assessment Questionnaires, inventories, workbooks, programs) available for use by engaged couples alone or in the context of therapeutic or pastoral premarital counseling, it is wise to be discerning about which materials to use. For a brief review of some of these resources, see Appendix 6.

We are not alone in this work. We are called to take the time to explore which educational strategies and resources for doing premarital counseling are available for our particular settings of ministry.

Now we are ready to craft a design for pastoral premarital counseling that addresses the important topic of domestic violence.

CHAPTER FIVE
ADDRESSING DOMESTIC VIOLENCE IN PREMARITAL COUNSELING

With the informational and theological foundations in place, we turn to concrete strategies. How do we routinely screen for domestic violence with individuals? And how can we most effectively include an educational discussion of both healthy covenantal relationships and of domestic violence prevention in our premarital sessions with couples, while simultaneously remaining alert to possible signs of abuse?

All of this must be done very carefully. Dealing with domestic violence is complex and can be dangerous. With this essential principle in mind, this chapter offers the "how to" for addressing domestic violence in these three important ways – routine screening with individuals, educating couples about healthy covenantal relationships, and educating/raising awareness about domestic violence with couples while watching for patterns that might indicate abuse (either actual or potential).

For these tasks, the following guidelines are important:

- ▶ The number one goal in screening for domestic violence is safety for the victim.

- ▶ Keeping confidences is essential in our role as pastors. Information shared in conversations is to be kept inviolate unless permission is granted by the person from whom the information came, or if there is concern for the physical safety of one or both partners. It is our responsibility to keep confidences to protect the safety of the victim. We also bear responsibility to confront the abuser and hold him accountable for his violent behavior, *as long as we will not be endangering the victim by doing so.*[14]

- ▶ Couples' counseling is never appropriate in relationships where there is violence, the fear or threat of violence, or where any type of abuse is present.

- Many victims of domestic violence need to hear repeatedly what domestic violence is and how it is experienced before they are able to name it for themselves and seek appropriate help. This process can take a long time. As pastors we are to do what we can, with patient diligence, to bring help and healing to victims and accountability for abusers.

- At any point in premarital counseling when information about abuse is revealed or suspected, or one or both partners do not appear to be participating in good faith in the process, a pastor may responsibly withdraw from officiating at the wedding (see Chapter Six for strategies).

To summarize, these are our tasks related to domestic violence with couples in premarital counseling:

- Communicate why we believe awareness and discussion of domestic violence should be included in premarital counseling.

- Routinely screen for current or potential abuse with partners in individual sessions.

- Watch and listen for any signs of current or potential abuse with couples together.

- Respond appropriately when domestic violence is disclosed or suspected.

- Offer education in couples' sessions – teaching about healthy covenantal relationships and educating about the dynamics of domestic violence – as an integral part of the process.

Part 1: Screening for Past, Current or Potential Domestic Violence with Individual Partners of a Couple

Routine screening for domestic violence with individual partners is an essential part of premarital counseling and should take place relatively early in the process. This is a step that needs to happen routinely with *all* couples. It is our opportunity to ask directly about abuse in the relationship.

As we meet with each partner separately, our task is to create a safe and confidential setting to screen for past, current or potential domestic violence by asking direct, matter-of-fact, yes/no questions. It is critical that we meet with each partner alone, without friends or family members present. Using language that is appropriate to the particular person's culture and context, maintaining an open, nonjudgmental tone of voice and a pastoral presence of integrity and compassion, these questions should explore:

- Abuse in family of origin.

- Abuse in past relationships.

- Concerns about the potential for violence in this relationship: fear of abuse; concerns about expressing anger; explosive episodes, controlling or dominating behavior.

- Current or past abuse in this relationship – physical, emotional or sexual.[15]

Here are a series of questions to use in an individual screening session during premarital counseling. As is clear from these questions, the primary dynamic to watch for is *control over* a partner, which can result in a variety of abusive behaviors (as described in Chapter Three).

- Do you feel that your partner doesn't take you seriously when you're talking together by laughing at you or putting down you or your ideas?

- Does your partner want to control what you do or where you go?

- Does your partner want to make all the decisions?

- Does your partner control your finances, make you turn over your money to him/her when you don't want to?

- Does your partner want to know where you are every minute of the day?

- Does your partner monitor your phone?

- Is your partner jealous of time you spend with friends, family or other relationships?

- Does your partner limit your time with family or friends?

- Is your partner hard to please, irritable, demanding, critical?

- Does your partner call you names or yell at you?

- Does your partner threaten deportation or take charge of your visa?

- Do you ever feel afraid of or threatened by your partner?

- Has your partner ever threatened or injured your pet, or forced you not to feed your pet or to neglect it in other ways?

- Has your partner forced you to give your pet away?

- Has your partner ever destroyed or threatened to destroy something that you valued?

- Have you ever been forced by your partner to have sexual activities when you did not want to?

- Describe how you and your partner each handle angry feelings. Do you feel comfortable with the way your partner deals with anger?

- Have you ever been hit, slapped, choked, kicked, restrained or otherwise hurt by your partner?[16]

If the answer to any of these questions is "yes" and you begin to have a concern for the safety of this person, the immediate priority is to express that concern, assess safety for the victim and provide appropriate support, using the strategies suggested in Chapter Six. The questions listed on page 46 will help you assess the level of intensity of the abuse and the degree of danger to the victim.

The above questions are intended to help identify *victims* of domestic violence in the context of premarital counseling. I have also found that, given a unique pastoral relationship of trust and understanding, it is sometimes possible (although not common) that abusers or potential abusers may disclose their own violent behavior. For this reason, I have included additional exploratory questions for individual screening sessions. It is important to note that the following questions would not be appropriate if the other partner has already disclosed abuse or fear of abuse in an individual session. These questions include:

- What do you do when you are frustrated and angry with your partner?

- Do you ever feel your anger with your partner gets "out of hand"?

- What aspects of your relationship cause you to feel "out of control" – money, time with family or friends, jealousy of your partner's friendships, your partner's career?

- How do you move from a feeling of rage to a calmer way of being with your partner?

- When you consider other marriages in your friendship circle or in your family, what do you think will be your own biggest challenge as you embark on this journey of covenant love with your partner?

CHAPTER FIVE

- Have you ever damaged your partner's property or pet?
- Have you ever threatened your partner with physical harm?
- Has your partner ever been afraid of you?
- Have you ever physically hurt your partner?

Responses to these questions, when assessed in conjunction with the prior questions and conversations with the couple together, will offer the pastor another kind of information about the possibility of domestic violence within the relationship.

Experienced clergy who have worked with victims and perpetrators of domestic violence give a helpful word of caution when asking direct questions in the screening process. For one thing, engaged persons may manifest a particular "blindness" when asked to reflect on their own experiences or patterns of behavior. They may be too caught up in the rush of being "in love" to name fears or doubts about the relationship or about a power imbalance. Another reality is that abusers often present well in conversations – seemingly engaged in the process, articulate but not entirely candid about behaviors, and apparently eager to please the pastor who is guiding the discussion. Once again, we are to trust our intuition, listen for information, watch for signs, and nurture our pastoral relationships with couples to maximize the possibility that individuals will be as open and honest as possible.

Part 2: Educating and Raising Awareness with Couples about Healthy Covenantal Relationships and about Domestic Violence

As we meet with couples, the following steps are important: affirming the components of healthy covenantal relationships, naming domestic violence as a significant topic for premarital discussion, sharing information and raising awareness about the nature and dynamics of domestic violence, and watching and listening for possible signs of abuse in the relationship.

CHAPTER FIVE

Goals in Meeting with Couples Together

▶ *Affirm the components of life-giving covenantal relationships.*

One of our primary tasks in premarital counseling is to invite couples to explore their loving partnerships in the light of God's covenant with God's people. We can use a variety of exercises, homework assignments, conversation topics and handouts to accomplish this task. Topics might include: values, family of origin issues, communication (listening, speaking, working through conflict, understanding feelings, nonverbal aspects, safety of expression, expressing appreciation, etc.), roles and expectations, religious/spiritual factors, vocation, money, extended family, and power dynamics – in addition to planning the wedding service. Using Handout #6, "What Ties or Severs the Covenant" (page 82), and Handout #7, "Contrasting Contractual and Covenantal Relationships" (page 84), can be a helpful way to set a beginning context with couples so that they become acquainted with the notion of covenant. This framework promotes healthy relationship dynamics and provides couples with the tools for moving through conflicts and differences with mutual respect and regard for shared power.

▶ *Name domestic violence as a significant topic for premarital discussion.*

This sends a clear message from the pastor to the couple. That message is: "My denomination, this church and I believe that when two people promise to mutually love, protect and care for one another in a sacred covenant with God, there is no place for violence or abuse. If one partner breaks this trust by using abuse or violence, your marriage covenant is broken. There is nothing in any religious teachings, including scripture and doctrine, that justifies or excuses domestic violence. That's why I believe it is extremely important for all couples – in all circumstances, ages, socioeconomic backgrounds and faith traditions – to ponder this topic very seriously."

Another pastoral message that might be shared is this: "None of us wants to think that we will ever have a problem with domestic violence. However, statistics indicate that abuse occurs in more marriages and intimate relationships than we would imagine, one in four. Each of those relationships in which abuse occurred began with some degree of mutual love and appreciation. Something went terribly wrong. Partners – mostly women, sometimes men – were hurt in many ways. The fact is that anyone can be a victim or a perpetrator of violence. Even though every story is

CHAPTER FIVE

different, I believe it is my responsibility to share as much information as I can to acquaint you with domestic violence and to urge your own honest reflections on the topic."

In addressing this issue, we all have our own unique styles, our own theological interpretations and ways of expressing ourselves. What is essential is that we be clear and heartfelt when we open this door with engaged couples.

▶ *Share information and raise awareness.*

A handout for couples, including definitions, statistics, suggestions of "What to do if you are experiencing abuse," plus phone numbers of local domestic violence programs, is a good start. (See Handout #3, "What Every Couple Needs to Know," page 76, for sample of an information page.) Written, concise information is more effective than just speaking about the topic. Reviewing an information page carefully with the couple is even more effective than merely handing it to them and hoping they'll read it later. As you review the information, watch and listen pastorally, invite questions, and perhaps ask if they have known any experiences of domestic violence among their families or circle of friends. In such story telling, you might follow up with a question or two like these:

- How did that experience affect their relationship?
- How did the victim find support?
- How did you feel and what did you do when you learned of this?
- What were the consequences of this event/experience for that couple? For their families? Their friends?
- What do you imagine you would do if this happened in your marriage?
- What do you believe couples should know and understand about domestic violence from your experience of witnessing this event?

▶ *Watch and listen for signs of current or potential abuse.*

As we educate about domestic violence with both partners of a couple together, we will also have the opportunity to observe their patterns of communication and interaction. If we remain aware, we may notice behavior that indicates a consistent pattern of control of one partner by the other, alerting us to the possibility of current or potential future abuse.

There are some particular warning signs or "red flags" in couple sessions that should alert us to the possibility of domestic violence:

- An inordinate need on the part of one of the partners to control the conversation, interrupt, or pontificate on answers to pastoral questions.

- A self-demeaning hesitation by one partner to participate in the conversation, deferring in a frightened manner to the partner, or looking at the partner for approval before answering.

- Extreme irritation, agitation or fear expressed in words and body language when the topic of domestic violence is raised.

- Inappropriate use of humor, putdowns, discounting responses, bullying, sarcasm, impatience.

- Repeated disagreements in which one partner is easily angered.

- Indications of jealousy, attempt to control the partner's responses, an attitude of disrespect.

In couples' sessions, questions that can be answered "yes" or "no" are not as effective as questions that begin with "how" or "what." Because abusers often react violently when their partners report domestic violence, it is important not to ask a direct question such as, "Has either of you ever hurt the other when you became angry?" in the context of couples' sessions. More appropriate *indirect and open-ended* questions can be used as we deal with some of the related topics generally covered in the couples' sessions of pastoral premarital counseling.

Entry Points for Discussion of Domestic Violence

We all have our lists of essential topics and strategies to cover in premarital counseling, developed on our own or collected from training sessions, resources and colleagues. Several topics are natural entry points for a focus on domestic violence, once we look through this special lens. Four of these topics are included here: values, family of origin, communication skills/conflict resolution, and role definitions/expectations. Introduction of these topics provides an opportunity to discuss the components of healthy covenantal relationships, to educate about domestic violence, and to be alert for signs of potential abuse in the relationship. Handouts #4 and #5, "Power and Control Wheel" and

CHAPTER FIVE

"Equality Wheel" (pages 78 and 80), are appropriate for use with any of these four topics.

Values

As we explore values with engaged couples, we are affirming the central theme of covenantal relationships: we are created by God as unique and special individuals with particular gifts and skills, behaviors and beliefs. When we fall/grow in love with another, we continue to be two interesting and unique persons, each committed to honor the uniqueness of the beloved other. Engaged partners, looking at this aspect of their relationship, will discover that they are alike in some values and that they differ in others. In a covenantal relationship, it is assumed that partners do not have to agree on all values, but they should respect and honor one another and seek to understand each other's deeply-held values.

Affirming each partner's individuality as a gift of God dispels the dangerous myth that married partners must agree on everything, a myth that is not possible to live out, and which may cause great distress if taken to be the goal. In exploring the topic of values with engaged couples, I often invite their response to several true vignettes of married couples in which values are expressed: "If this happened in your marriage, would you be comfortable or challenged?" The vignettes I include cover a wide range of issues – saving/spending money, spiritual expression/religious involvement, career/vocation, and children/family participation, among others. As two partners listen to one another respond to the vignettes, they begin to see that it is common to interpret life events differently, and that such differences do not need to be threatening to the covenant bond. In fact, different perspectives are to be celebrated as partners seek to know and understand one another more fully. Affirming those values that are held in common (about marriage and their joint commitment to one another), while simultaneously delighting in the authentic uniqueness of each person – this is one of the great gifts of covenant love!

As couples engage in this discussion of values, we may be aware of resistance to the affirmation that two persons who love each other can hold different values. One or both partners may repeatedly maintain, "Oh, we're in love…we see everything exactly the same way. We have the same likes and dislikes, the same hopes and dreams, the same reactions to stress. We agree on everything." This would be a small "red flag" to note as we look at the potential for domestic violence. This kind of articulated self-assessment may portend disaster the first time a couple experiences a difference in opinion or perspective. Generally, a guided conversation about values is a good way to sense how realistic a couple is in their own self-definition, how safe each partner is to express his or her perspective, and how mutually respectful partners are when dealing with their unique views of life, love, and the world around them. When safety, mutual respect, and the other aspects of covenant love are not present, it is possible that one partner may be dominating or controlling the other…a behavior that could signal the possibility of current or future abuse.

Family of Origin

Couples do not fall/grow in love in a vacuum. As we know, partners bring the learnings (for better or for worse) from their family and relational histories to their decision to join together in covenant love. Inviting couples to reflect on these histories is a significant part of premarital counseling.

There are various ways to do this. I invite partners, in a solitary activity, to use colored markers to draw the families in which they lived when they were about ten years old (including themselves in the picture) – on big newsprint. (This does not have to be a fancy picture; it can be simple stick figures.) Colors can be used to indicate which family member was warm, who made decisions, who was funny, who was distant, who connected with whom, and where the power was lodged. Then I guide them as they review their pictures with each other, focusing on their major learnings about covenant love from their experience (sometimes painful, sometimes great, often mixed), and exploring those dynamics that they hope will be similar and those that might be different in their own newly created covenant.

I invite partners to ask questions of each other in exploring their learnings from their families of origin. Major themes are revealed in this conversation: relationship to drugs and alcohol, religious/faith traditions, norms, attitudes and behaviors about how a loving family thrives (or not), and others. This exploration affirms that covenant partners carry with them histories and learnings, which must be embraced as part of married life together.

Patterns of domestic violence can sometimes be traced to family history. Another strategy I've used when exploring the experiences of loving and being loved (or not) in each partner's family of origin, includes asking some of the following questions:

- Describe how decisions were made in the family in which you grew up.

- How and by whom was conflict handled?

CHAPTER FIVE

- How would you describe the relationship between your mother and father? What characteristics in your parents' marriage do you admire? What characteristics in their marriage were/are difficult for you?

- What happened in your family when someone got mad at another family member? How was anger expressed?

- In what ways are you like your father/mother?

- When your family gets together, is there anyone you need to worry about?

- What were the family values about religion, use of alcohol and drugs, expressions of affection and disappointment, work and leisure, discipline, etc.?

- What methods of disciplining children were used in your family of origin?

- If you could change anything about your parents' marriage, what would that be?

- As you think about methods of handling conflict, in what ways are/were your parents' marriage similar to or different from that of your partner's parents?

- What was the most helpful learning from your family of origin which each of you brings into your marriage (related to either a positive or a challenging dynamic)?

Family of origin explorations allow us to reflect on learnings and to enhance the possibility for life-giving relationships. In addition, if we are listening and watching pastorally to couple and partner responses, we can begin to identify relational patterns emerging from the family story that may reveal a history of or potential for abuse.

Communication Skills/Conflict Resolution

The daily sacred work of covenant life occurs in the communications – verbal and nonverbal – between partners. When contrasted with communications between contracted parties or between persons in casual relationships, covenantal communications are refreshingly different. (See Handout #2, "Covenantal Communications," page 74.) The task for the pastor in premarital counseling is to lift up the dynamics of covenantal communications, provide a setting for practicing skills, and encourage honest reflection. In my experience, this can be the most rewarding groundwork of all premarital counseling, as couples look together at these questions:

- How do we learn and practice covenantal communications?
- What does it mean to listen with an open heart and a respectful presence?
- How do we speak the truth in love rather than assume we have "The Truth?"
- How might we work through conflicts with mutual respect, engaging in a process that encourages both partners to listen and speak and then work together toward a resolution so that each partner can let go of the need to control the outcome?
- How can we live with the reality that often couples need to agree to disagree?
- How do we make decisions together that honor our different perspectives?
- How safe are we to express our opinions, share our views with each other?
- How well do we communicate our appreciation to and for one another?
- How is humor a dynamic in our relationship? When does it draw us closer together? When does it distance us from each other?

In my experience, when engaged couples begin to see alternative ways to speak and listen and communicate, the notion of covenant comes alive in a profound way and partners are inspired to give their covenant life daily attention.

Exploring styles of conflict resolution gives us an opportunity to observe the relationship dynamics and to watch for possible patterns of control. Inviting a couple to describe a recent conflict and how they worked it through is a helpful way to approach this topic. If the couple shares in the response, we learn a bit about their style of communicating. Is it a mutual one of openness to each other's perceptions? If one partner responds most of the time, it is important to confirm what has been shared with the other partner: "Is this how you saw things? Did you see anything differently? Would you add anything to your partner's description of this situation?"

Another open-ended way to gather information about a couple's decision-making style is to ask the question, "How do you come to a joint decision when you disagree on something?"

CHAPTER FIVE

A further way to assess potential for domestic violence is to explore expressions of anger. Posing one or two questions such as those listed below can be helpful:

- We all experience anger, frustration and even rage from time to time. How does each of you express these emotions?

- Describe how you are when you are at your best with each other in a stressful situation.

- Describe how you are when you are at your worst with each other in a stressful situation.

- When you are upset, what would you like your partner to do or say?

Some colleagues have shared a sense of inadequacy when the topic of anger is explored. One minister describes an incident when a man, in responding to these questions, said, "Well, I do have a bit of an anger management problem." My colleague said he was inclined to acknowledge that briefly and then move along to topics that were a bit more comfortable for him.

Staying in comfortable territory is sometimes tempting in our pastoral work, but this disclosure is an excellent example of a door opening to further exploration of the couple's power dynamics and the potential for abuse. By attuning carefully to comments and/or behaviors, we can open the door to this important pastoral conversation.

Handout #8 ,"Constructive and Destructive Ways of Dealing with Anger" (page 86), is yet another recommended strategy in a guided conversation with an engaged couple on the topic of anger.

As we use our own particular pastoral styles in these encounters with couples, and as we learn more about the devastating reality of domestic violence and what we can do to prevent it, we might need to trust ourselves to "read" situations with more confidence. If we are helping couples develop skills for working through conflicts with mutual respect, we can pick up clues, in even the briefest of exchanges or the shortest of comments, exposing potential issues of power, control, or domination, which should then inform the work that follows.

One highly respected pastoral counselor uses this approach when dealing with anger in premarital counseling:

> We all feel angry from time to time. We are responsible for how our anger gets expressed. I'm asking you to make a promise to each other before your wedding, in writing and verbally, that when you get angry, you will not hit,

slap, grab, shove, or block the other person. When you are angry you have permission to call a "time out" and your partner must grant it.[17]

This counselor addresses the topic after three sessions with the couple and after having completed some work on communication and conflict resolution. He invites observations about each individual's own anger and that of his/her partner. He also guides the couple in a conversation about how they might work with their anger in constructive ways.

Role Definitions and Expectations

How engaged couples see themselves as mutual caretakers of one another's bodies and souls, and as partners in the adventure of covenant life, is yet another important topic to be included in pastoral premarital counseling. As God cares lovingly for God's people, so couples are called to care for one another and to share the daily tasks of living with a spirit of gratitude and mutual responsibility. I've found that this topic is best explored in the posing of questions (see below). Another strategy is asking an engaged couple to describe a married couple they know well, with a particular eye toward their roles and responsibilities: "How are each partner's roles negotiated? Do you think each partner has an equal voice in the conversation? What would you like to emulate in this couple's relationship? What troubles you about their marriage?" Couples often learn about their own dynamics by observing the dynamics of other couples; this can be a useful teaching strategy.

Inviting a couple to engage in a conversation related to life dreams, hopes and values can reveal much about their views of vocations and careers, money, religious faith, politics, recreational interests, household maintenance and if/how each has the freedom to express his/her individuality in these arenas of shared life. By participating in and observing these conversations, we are able to note such dynamics as gender biases, power differentials, freedom of expression, mutual respect, etc., all of which help us informally assess the presence of or potential for domestic violence.

(Although some engaged couples live together before marriage, we cannot assume this is the experience for every couple. Designing these questions to fit specific couples is important.)

- How will you design a budget? Who will pay the bills?

- Describe what you share about religious faith and where you disagree. How will your church commitment be expressed?

- How do household chores get done?
- How would you describe a man's role in a marriage? A woman's role?
- What are your expectations for the man's role and the woman's role in disciplining children?
- If both partners have career goals, how will you decide whose career is most important?
- What volunteer opportunities are exciting for you?
- What are your expectations of marriage? Of your role as a marriage partner?
- What dimensions of covenant life will be challenging for you to live out?
- Describe three recent experiences of "give and take," when you felt you were participants in a mutual covenantal relationship.
- How do you experience a mutual sharing of power without "keeping score?"

Other topics in couples' sessions that are possible entry points for introducing the subject of domestic violence include:

- Exploring the myths of marriage (including the idea that partners will change after they are married).
- Planning for budget and financial future (the number one reason for marital conflict).
- Support for the marital journey from extended family and friends (see Handout #1, "Covenant Circles of Support," page 72).

In each of these topics, couples can begin to articulate their own commitments to sustaining a healthy life together. In addition, appropriate questions can reveal power inequities and control issues between partners, which can be indicators of abuse.

Other helpful tools and exercises intended to offer support for healthy covenantal relationships and to explore the presence of or potential for domestic violence are included in the Appendices and the Handouts at the end of this book.

CHAPTER FIVE

As we do this important and challenging pastoral work, Isaiah's words remind us of our calling.

> I heard the voice of the Holy One saying, "Whom shall I send, and who will go for us?" Then I said, "Here I am! Send me!" How wonderful it is to see a messenger coming across the mountains, bringing good news, the news of peace! The messenger announces victory and says to Zion, "Your God reigns." The Spirit of God is upon me, because the Holy One has anointed me to bring good news to the poor, heal the brokenhearted, proclaim liberty to the captives, and freedom to those who are bound.
>
> (Isaiah 61:1) [18]

CHAPTER SIX

WHAT TO DO WHEN DOMESTIC VIOLENCE IS DISCLOSED OR SUSPECTED IN PREMARITAL COUNSELING[19]

As we include the topic of domestic violence in various ways throughout our premarital counseling, we are educators as well as pastors. Couples will – at the very least – understand that covenantal relationships are a gift from a gracious God and need to be tended with respect and care each and every day. They will also begin to learn about domestic violence and will understand that there is no place for abuse in covenantal relationships.

Sometimes, as we screen individually for domestic violence, one or both partners may share with us the painful truth that it is already present in their relationship. Or, when we meet with both partners together, if we have provided the setting and the information carefully and thoughtfully, we may learn or suspect that abuse is present or we may be concerned about the potential for future violence.

At first, we will probably want to dismiss these concerns, hoping that what we've heard and seen just wasn't true or that, by the next session, things will somehow magically be all right. After all, this is the time for emphasizing the positive and for finishing the wedding planning…and besides, the wedding is already on the church calendar!

As we have learned, however, we have a responsibility, to all with whom we work, to do whatever we can to affirm life rather than death – whether physical or spiritual. And so, once again, it is important to proceed carefully, clearly and in a timely manner, keeping in mind that the safety of the victim is at stake. Remember during this phase that when a partner tries to break away from an abuser, the chance of the violence escalating increases markedly.

When Domestic Violence is Disclosed Directly

When domestic violence is disclosed directly in an individual session, our steps for pastoral action are the following:

▶ *Take the disclosure seriously.*

Be a good listener as you hear the facts and feelings that are being shared with you. It may be very challenging for us to believe and accept that a person with whom we may have worked for years in the church, who seems so charming and helpful, is capable of doing the things his partner is disclosing. But victims rarely lie about or exaggerate such behavior, and it is critical that we believe them. An appropriate first pastoral response might be this: "Judy, I am so sorry to hear that Jack has done several things which are scary to you. Given the information you've shared with me about how he has kept you from seeing your friends, his insistence that he know everything you're doing every minute of the day, and the fact that he shoved you away from the phone last week, you have every reason to be frightened. I think you may be in danger."

▶ *Discern the level of intensity of the actual violence or threat of violence.*

After there has been an indication that abuse is present in a relationship, the level of intensity of actual violence or threat of violence can be evaluated by using the following questions.[20] *Ask these questions first to determine if an immediate crisis exists.*

- Do you feel you are in immediate danger tonight?
- Are you afraid to go home to your partner after our meeting (or to see your partner if you do not live together)?
- Can you describe a recent event when you were frightened by your partner's behavior?
- Does the violence seem to be getting worse?

If the answer to one or more of these questions is "yes" and you feel that an urgent crisis exists, take these steps while she is in your office:

› Assure her that you believe her story, are concerned for her safety and will help her find support to take whatever actions she chooses to protect herself.

› Help connect her with a professional domestic violence crisis advocate by telephone in your office. The National Domestic Violence Hotline at 800-799-7233 will have an advocate available to talk with her and will also be able to give her the phone

CHAPTER SIX

number of a local shelter or domestic violence agency in your area. The advocate will be able to explain the options available to her and help her develop a plan to ensure her safety.

> Remind her that you will not share the information she has given you with the alleged abuser or anyone else.

If it is determined that abuse is present in the relationship, but the victim does not believe she is in immediate danger, you may wish to respond in this way: "Joan, in our session together you've shared some important information and experiences with me about how Hal has been treating you. I appreciate your courage, candor and trust. Some of the most disturbing behaviors are these: … (retell what she has said, using her own words). I have a real concern for your well-being because, although you may not think this is a "big deal" and Hal apologizes and feels badly after each event, it sounds like the violent episodes are increasing in number and severity. As your pastor, I'm concerned that a dangerous pattern is emerging which places you in an unsafe position. I care about you and know that what you have shared with me is alarming enough to warrant some expert advice for you. I'll help you with that."

Offering support and strategies to keep the victim safe, assisting her in acknowledging the reality of her abusive circumstances, and helping her make critical decisions are the primary pastoral goals at this stage.

> Make sure the victim has correct information about local shelters, hotlines and support resources and help her assess her current situation and plan of action. To protect her safety, this needs to be done with her privately and without her partner's knowledge. (Note that phone or email messages are not options under these circumstances.) Connecting the victim to an advocate immediately by telephone in your office is one way to reassure her that there is caring, knowledgeable help available. The National Domestic Violence Hotline (a confidential, toll-free service at 800-799-7233) has advocates available 24 hours/day and will also be able to connect you or her with a local domestic violence program in your community.

> Help her develop a safety plan. A safety plan is a way by which she can try to protect herself or attempt to leave home quickly should she feel she is in danger. It may include knowing how to

reach a taxi, having cash ready, and/or having a way to be in touch with a trusted friend to help her in a crisis.

In both of these scenarios, it is critical, for the safety of the victim, that you not approach the abuser or tell anyone else about what has been shared with you about her situation.

▶ *Support the victim by letting her know that the abuse is not her fault, that she is not alone, that God does not want her to suffer, and that you will be present to help support her in dealing with the situation.*

▶ *Decide that you cannot, in good faith, officiate at the wedding.*

We've all had experiences of guiding couples both before and during a wedding service with the best of our skills, only to be left with a sense of disquiet about the future of their covenant journeys as we bid them "Godspeed" at the close of the wedding service. Some of us may also have had the experience of sharing concerns and suggesting postponement of the wedding plans, in order for the couple to do some further counseling. When I've experienced the latter, my cautions have usually been related to particularly challenging conflicts the couple is facing without resolution – e.g., unresolved family of origin or communication issues which seem to impair joyful and healthy living, physical or emotional health concerns, or a seeming disregard for the process of premarital counseling and wedding planning. In most cases, the couples involved appear to have understood and respected my advice and followed through with suggestions (although I may have found this out much later).

However, when it comes to evidence of current or potential domestic violence or serious power imbalance with an engaged couple, I believe there is only one appropriate response. If there is any hint of abuse now or in the future, it is our responsibility to decline from officiating at the wedding.

Some pastors – because of their awareness of domestic violence and its high incidence, as well as other possible destructive relationship dynamics – do not commit to officiate at a wedding before marriage counseling begins. One such pastor writes about her process this way:

> I tell couples up front that the journey of premarital counseling is something we all embark on together, to see whether I should be the one to perform their wedding service. Thus, I leave myself the option

CHAPTER SIX

to back out of performing the marriage if I have serious concerns. A power imbalance in the relationship is one reason why I would consider declining to perform the ceremony. When I have enough real concerns, I decline to continue to work with them on the wedding. In declining, I specify the reason, but in cases where I suspect domestic violence, I have to do this in a way that is safe. Thus, I may talk to the less powerful partner privately, and then state a more general reason when talking to the couple together. I know that they may find someone else to perform the ceremony, but I think it is important for someone to have raised concerns and to have acted on those concerns. [21]

It is wise to have a plan that is consistently shared with all engaged couples so that they understand what will be happening throughout the process of premarital counseling and what the pastor's role will be.

▶ *Share this decision and the reasons for it with the victim partner in an individual session.*

It is important to use language that communicates respect, care, and concern at all times, but especially during this difficult time. Here is one way I've done this:

"As we have worked together over these weeks, Mary, I have come to be concerned about some of the dynamics in your relationship. They are of such concern that I need to share them with you now, before we go any further in our premarital counseling. My major concern is that Fred seems to treat you in ways that are extremely disrespectful and might even be hurtful – emotionally and possibly physically. He is using many of the attitudes and behaviors we talked about when we looked at the components of domestic violence two sessions ago. Frankly, I'm so concerned about your well-being in this relationship that I feel I cannot, in good faith, officiate at your wedding at this time. Fred needs to acknowledge his harmful behavior, seek help, and commit to doing the hard work necessary to make meaningful change. I care deeply about you and about your hopes and dreams for a happy marriage, and I don't see that those dreams are possible, given what I've witnessed as we've met together.

"This is difficult for me to share with you because I value your family's presence in this congregation and your wedding plans are well underway. I know it may be difficult for you to hear this. But I've prayed and thought about what I've seen and heard, and I feel this is what I must tell you at this time. My calling as your pastor is to speak the truth in love to you and to help you live the abundant life Jesus spoke about — whether you are alone or in a relationship. I do not see that happening right now. You are too special a person and marriage is too significant a relationship for me to be quiet at this point. Because I care about you, I will help you find resources, counseling, safety and support as you proceed. I will help you cancel the wedding service or postpone it indefinitely, until you have received the support you need and Fred has taken responsibility for his behavior, sought help, and demonstrated real change."

Key components of this kind of message are candor, pastoral presence, clarity and support for next steps.

▶ *Make a plan with the victim partner for next steps, with respect to the premarital counseling and wedding planning that will ensure her safety.*

Discuss strategies with her for discontinuing premarital counseling, postponing or canceling the wedding service, advising the abusive partner of resources and responsibilities, and dealing with family and friends. Not only is it important for the victim to agree with suggested strategies; it is essential that she know which of these tasks you will do and which you will help her accomplish by finding other resources to support her.

▶ *Depending on the victim partner's sense of safety and well-being, the pastor's decision not to officiate and accompanying suggestions should be shared — either with the couple together or with the abusive partner individually.*

If, in the separate session, the potential victim expresses a sense of sufficient safety and a desire for the pastor to share this decision with the couple together, then a final session with both partners is appropriate and the couple may be told together that you cannot, in good conscience, officiate at their wedding until and unless some major work related to the possibility of domestic violence is completed by the abusive partner. This will need to take place in a specialized batterers' intervention program. If the victim indicates that it would be unsafe for her to participate in a session in which domestic violence is named, you should then be sure of the victim's safety first and proceed to tell her partner that you cannot officiate because of some more general reasons (e.g., "I feel you need to work on your communication patterns," or some other similar approach).

CHAPTER SIX

- *Stop couples' sessions.*

- *If, and only if, you can be sure of the safety of the victim, advise the abuser (usually the man) that he needs to connect with a local skilled resource (give names, addresses, and phone numbers of batterers' intervention programs) to engage in a process of learning how his behaviors and attitudes have caused a climate of fear, danger and mistrust in the relationship and what he can do to change.*

- *Assure both partners that God loves them and wants them to live in joy and health, and that you will help them find the appropriate support to do so.*

- *Do not continue counseling with the victim or the abuser unless you have been trained to do so.*

- *Do not promise a particular outcome, such as forgiveness or reconciliation. Stay with the present needs for canceling/postponing the wedding, connecting with resources, and assuring the safety of the victim.*

- *Do not expect an enthusiastic response to the information you are sharing with engaged couples. Individually or as a couple, they may be hurt, angry, puzzled and defensive. It often takes great patience over time to work with these complex situations.*

Another dimension of the pastor's task will be to follow through with the couple and the family as they respond to this decision. Once again, confidentiality is important and the safety of the victim partner is primary, so we are called to do this work respectfully, compassionately and faithfully. Couples (and their families) may be disappointed, angry, upset and puzzled by a pastor's decision not to officiate. Some couples, as we know, move along to another church and find another pastor to proceed with a wedding service. But many welcome the chance to stop the wedding planning, while they find help and healing for the victim and support for potential change for the abuser.

You will want to develop your own response, articulating these points in whatever way is appropriate for you, keeping in mind, as always, that differences in culture, ethnicity, class, and faith backgrounds will affect how you respond to the couple and how they interpret what you share.

> ### IMPORTANT INFORMATION FOR PASTORS
>
> *When we feel we could be in danger:*
>
> If, in the midst of a session with a couple, we feel highly anxious about our own safety or that of one of the partners, we are advised to take a break. Call for a "time out."
>
> Our primary task in the midst of a disclosure process is to access the domestic violence experts or experienced colleagues for recommended safety procedures, possible police involvement and advocacy. Having information about local resources or the National Domestic Violence Hotline (1-800-799-SAFE) close at hand is essential.
>
> We are trained as pastors, not as domestic violence experts. Whenever we have a question about how to proceed in premarital – or other – couples' counseling because of anxiety about safety, we need to seek and follow the advice of those who know what to do.

When Domestic Violence is Suspected

If your observations of the partners' interactions lead you to suspect domestic violence but it is not directly disclosed to you, or if the suspected victim denies that abuse is a reality, the following are the appropriate steps:

- The pastor needs to express her/his concern honestly and compassionately with the suspected victim. While expressing concern for the victim's safety, the pastor may indicate that s/he may not be the right pastor to officiate at her wedding unless this concern is acknowledged openly and addressed appropriately.

- The pastor may also acknowledge that s/he may be wrong but it would be helpful if s/he could review some of the screening questions once again with the woman and provide support, depending on the issues that emerge during their conversation.

- The pastor might suggest that the victim reflect on these comments and call back the following day with a decision about how to proceed.

- As always, it is important that the suspected victim be given helpful local resource information and the assurance that you, her pastor, will be glad to help connect her to appropriate resources.

When we are concerned that violent behavior is present or possible in a relationship, (even when the partner has responded "No" to screening questions), it is wisest to proceed by withdrawing from officiating at the wedding and following through with other relevant steps outlined above: "I am sorry; from what I have observed and heard, I suspect that there is abuse going on in your relationship and unless this is addressed I may not be the right pastor to officiate at your wedding. I am concerned for your safety." A pastor's response to suspected domestic violence needs to focus on pastoral strategies that help name this reality if it is true and seek safety for the victim and support for change in the abuser.

Once a pastor has responded to suspected domestic violence with the couple using these strategies, s/he may need to provide follow-up pastoral response to the extended family and the faith community. Because these situations do not occur in a vacuum, pastoral interpretation, comfort and support for others related to the couple are important. It is understood, of course, that this will occur only in those cases where partners choose to share the information with others; it is not appropriate for the pastor to share such confidential information.

Dealing With Faith Dimensions of Domestic Violence[22]

In the process of responding to potential or actual domestic violence, we may be challenged with important questions from a partner, a member of the family, or a member of the congregation. Some common questions and beginning pastoral responses are these:

- *Why does God let this happen?*

    God has created us as human beings who are empowered and free to make choices about who and how we love. God does not control the world; God loves the world and wants us to love rather than harm one another.

- *Why didn't God stop him from hurting me?*

    God's power takes the form of loving and healing. God is not an all-powerful Being who is in charge of what people do with each other. God calls us to act with love in our relationships just as God loves us.

CHAPTER SIX

> *Shouldn't I just forgive him and go ahead with the wedding?*

Forgiveness only happens after some important actions on the part of the one who has hurt you – your fiancé. He must first acknowledge that his behaviors have been wrong and that he has hurt you. He must show that he is serious about changing his ways – which can only happen over a period of time. Just saying, "I'm sorry," is not enough to warrant your forgiveness.

> *Everyone gets mad. Why are you making such a big deal of this?*

The behaviors you have described are more about controlling you than about "getting mad" at you. Controlling behavior does not go away without a lot of work with a professional specially trained to address this issue. Controlling behavior is what domestic violence is about and it can start with small actions and become life threatening. It *is* a "big deal" that you and your fiancé's marriage covenant be free of fear or threat of this controlling behavior, which stifles love and life.

> *I thought we were supposed to suffer for love. Isn't that what Jesus did?*

Jesus came to free all people from suffering and to call us to help free others from suffering. Your suffering because of your fiancé's hurtful behavior is not helping you or him or your relationship become more healthy and loving. Your suffering is not bringing you or your fiancé closer to God or to Jesus; it is actually getting in the way of the love and new life that you are intended to experience in your relationship.

> *In my church and family growing up, I was told that the man is the head of the household. Isn't that what the Bible says?*

Nowhere in the Bible does it say that a woman should be beaten or injured by her husband. St. Paul does speak of husbands and wives living in mutual submission to the ways of Christ. Those ways are loving and healing and kind and gentle; they are not domineering or controlling or hurtful.

> *I keep trying to pray harder for God to tell me how I can make things better for him so he won't be so angry. God never answers.*

Sometimes we think we know how God should answer our prayers, so

CHAPTER SIX

we close our hearts to other answers which come from God in many and mysterious ways. Perhaps God's answer to your prayer is found in the information and conversations we've had about domestic violence in our sessions together. Perhaps God is giving you courage to say you cannot share life in a marriage covenant with someone who wants to control and hurt you. Perhaps God's answer is offering you support and healing and giving your fiancé support to change his ways. You are not responsible for your partner's behavior or moods or anger; he is. There are ways he can find new life with God's help and with the help of trusted professionals who have worked with others.

> *I know that he's just stressed out right now because of the wedding and preparations, but I know that God can work miracles and that he will change after we're married. Isn't that what love does?*

Yes, God's love can transform lives and relationships in powerful ways. We know from experience with other engaged and married couples, however, that controlling behavior tends to get worse over time after marriage; it does not just change for the better because you are married. Now is the time to be honest and deal with it.

Moving into pastoral conversations about God, the sacrificial nature of Jesus' life and death, forgiveness and reconciliation, good and evil and other topics pertaining to domestic violence and faith calls for continual refining of our theological foundations. We can no longer rely on old tried-and-true responses to such questions asked in more general contexts of our ministries. They may not suffice, for us or for those with whom we are ministering, in the face of the realities and tragedies of domestic violence.

To bring good news of the blessings of covenant life and to speak of freedom to those who are bound by the fear or presence of domestic violence – this is our task.

These pastoral conversations will be significant, and most likely, they will reshape our own beliefs. Some fine resources addressing the faith dimensions of domestic violence will be found in the Selected Resources and Appendices.

Because most of us have not been well trained to deal with the signs and consequences of domestic violence, we need to learn how to courageously respond to a cry for help – whether it is direct or indirect. We can best do this by studying resources, by talking with professionally trained domestic violence experts, by developing responsible premarital counseling processes that affirm covenant life and reject domestic violence, by participating in educational trainings, and by staying grounded in the biblical and theological call from the prophet Micah:

> God has told you what is good;
> and what does God require of you
> but to do justice, and to love kindness
> and to walk humbly with your God.
>
> (Micah 6:8)

CHAPTER SEVEN
KEEPING THE DOOR OPEN:
ONGOING STRATEGIES FOR COUPLES, CHURCHES AND PASTORS

The prophet Hosea inspired us as we began to open the door to address domestic violence in our pastoral premarital counseling. What we have seen and learned beyond that open door takes us to a larger picture.

Once again, we turn to Hosea,

> What are you waiting for? Return to your God!
> Commit yourself in love, in justice!
> Don't give up on God — ever!
>
> (Based on Hosea 12:6)[23]

To inspire us in this sacred work called ministry, there could be no clearer call: we are to commit ourselves to love and justice for all people and to not give up on God. This resource has been focused on doing just that, with and for couples who are seeking to live in covenant love. Our hope is that what we learn in doing this small task permeates throughout our ministries in all our various settings.

It takes courage to be forthright in our speaking, it takes commitment to ongoing prayer and study, and it takes imagination to envision a world in which God's intention for peaceful interactions – especially between covenant partners – calls us to action. It is our task, then, to:

- Offer ongoing encouragement for couples with whom we have worked to share both the joys and challenges of covenant life.

- Mobilize our churches and communities of faith to keep the door open to affirming covenant life and to addressing domestic violence.

- Seek ways, in our role as pastors, to include the tragic reality of domestic violence in all our settings for ministry.

Listed below are suggested strategies for addressing each of these areas.

Offer Ongoing Encouragement for Couples

> Keep in touch with married couples by note or phone, with reminders of the joys and responsibilities of covenant love. This will make it clear to them that you care for their continued well-being and are available should they want to call upon you. For example, I send Valentine's Day cards to all couples at whose weddings I've officiated for one or two years following their weddings. In the notes, I write out their vows and offer a blessing of encouragement for the journey.

> Invite couples who have been married within the past year or two to a reunion where, with refreshments and a warm welcome, they might participate in a marital "tune-up." This could include a review of topics covered in premarital counseling, group discussion, and a prayer or scripture reading.

> Offer marriage enrichment classes, workshops, gatherings in which important topics, including domestic violence, are addressed. Contracting with a local therapist or another skilled professional to lead such sessions can be helpful for pastors who feel stretched for time.

> From time to time, offer a special column for couples in your church newsletter, in which pithy advice, scriptures, and notices of community events related to marriage might be shared as an indication of the church's commitment to life-giving marriage and family life.

> Offer support groups for couples in which they might explore, in mutual confidentiality and trust, the joys and the challenges of daily covenant life. Leadership might be shared within the group, or provided by a pastor or therapist. Resources might be used to guide both the content and the process of such groups. Another option is a monthly topical focus introduced by different member couples. In addition, mentoring programs can be set up to pair experienced married couples with engaged or newly-married couples.

Mobilize Our Churches and Communities of Faith

- Promote active commitment (on the part of pastors and lay leaders) to the inclusion of domestic violence in preaching, adult education, and family life ministries – children, youth, intergenerational – on an ongoing basis. This should include naming domestic violence as a problem, providing education on the basic dynamics of domestic violence, and offering pastoral care to both victims and abusers.

- Include written, video and other resources on domestic violence in the church library and on websites, with regular opportunities for church leaders and members to become familiar with them. (See www.faithtrustinstitute.org for educational resources designed specifically for faith communities.)

- Connect with and visit a local domestic violence program or shelter; sexual and domestic violence advocacy group; city, county or state funded center for referral and treatment. Participate in education and advocacy efforts.

- Provide domestic violence brochures or information sheets with local crisis line phone numbers, access to shelters, brief definitions and suggested action steps for both victims and abusers in all church restrooms.

- Create liturgical occasions in which victims of domestic violence are remembered and prayed for (without mentioning specific names) and in which the well-being of couples and families is named and explored in scripture, music and prayer. (See www.sabbathofdomesticpeace.org for resources.)

- Work ecumenically with other churches to highlight domestic violence as an important issue and to offer education, information and healing for victims as part of our shared ministry.

Seek Ways, as Pastors, to Include the Reality of Domestic Violence in all Our Ministry Settings

- Participate frequently in classes and trainings that address domestic violence prevention and the appropriate pastoral response. Include the topic of domestic violence in peer support groups or clergy retreats – for education, reflection and discussion.

- Seek help from a therapist, when appropriate, for personal issues related to domestic violence.

CHAPTER SEVEN

- Nurture your own faith life with daily prayer, Bible study, writing or meditation.

- Provide leadership for lay members by naming domestic violence in sermons and liturgies, Bible studies, education, pastoral care and mission endeavors.

- If you have never met or worked with a victim/survivor of domestic violence, ask a colleague who has, or visit a chaplain who works with survivors of domestic violence. Hearing the stories of real people can make a difference in how we address this topic in our ministries.

Every time I lead a marriage preparation workshop,
    every time I meet with an engaged couple in my office,
        I see the faces of people who say they are ready to
            begin covenant journeys of joy and fulfillment.

It is a daunting but vitally significant task we take on in premarital counseling. For the sake of the couples with whom we work, and for the sake of their families and the world, we must do no less than commit ourselves in justice and love, and not give up on God's grace in our work. My hope is that this resource will provide an important first step in equipping you with the information, tools and courage for this task. Blessings and courage as you open this door.

NOTES

Preface

1. Unless otherwise noted, all Scriptural quotations are from *New Revised Standard Version Bible*, copyright 1989, Division of Christian Education of the National Council of Churches of Christ in the United States of America. Used by permission. All rights reserved.

Chapter One

2. Pamela Cooper-White, *The Cry of Tamar: Violence Against Women and the Church's Response* (Minneapolis: Fortress Press, 1995), p. 118.

Chapter Two

3. Note from the author: Some recent programs and movements related to marriage enrichment have included the word "covenant" in their titles. Both the contents of this book and my understanding of covenant theology were developed independently of the current "covenant marriage" movement and are not related to any particular movement or organization.

4. Marie M. Fortune, *Keeping the Faith: Guidance for Christian Women Facing Abuse* (San Francisco: HarperCollins, 1995), p. 16–17.

5. Reprinted from Robert Bly, *Loving a Woman in Two Worlds* (NY: HarperCollins, 1987), ©1987 Robert Bly. Used with permission of Robert Bly.

6. Reprinted from Alice Walker, *Revolutionary Petunias and Other Poems* (NY: Harcourt, 1973), ©1973 and renewed 2001 by Alice Walker. Reprinted by permission of Harcourt.

7. From *South Carolina Review* 34 (2), Spring 2002. Reprinted with permission of *South Carolina Review*.

Chapter Three

8. Adapted from definitions found on www.ncadv.org (used with permission of National Coalition Against Domestic Violence) and from C. Warshaw & A. Ganley, *Domestic Violence: Improving the Health Care Response to Domestic Violence* (San Francisco: Family Violence Prevention Fund, 1998).

9. Intimate Partner Violence: Fact Sheet (Atlanta: Centers for Disease Control and Prevention, National Center for Injury Prevention and Control, www.cdc.gov/ncipc/factsheets/ipvfacts.htm).

10. Adapted from Nancy Murphy, *God's Reconciling Love: A Pastor's Handbook on Domestic Violence* (Seattle: FaithTrust Institute, 2003), p. 14-15.

11. From the brochure, "What Every Congregation Needs to Know about Domestic Violence" (Seattle: FaithTrust Institute, 1993).

12. Adapted from the brochure, "What Every Congregation Needs to Know about Domestic Violence" (Seattle: FaithTrust Institute, 1993); the Sabbath of Domestic Peace website (www.sabbathofdomesticpeace.org); and from C. Warshaw & A. Ganley, *Domestic Violence: Improving the Health Care Response to Domestic Violence* (San Francisco: Family Violence Prevention Fund, 1998).

13. Nancy Murphy, *God's Reconciling Love* (Seattle: FaithTrust Institute, 1993) p. 14.

Chapter Five

14. See more on this topic in Carol J. Adams, *Woman Battering* (Minneapolis: Fortress Press, 1994), Chap. 5, "Accountability."

15. Adapted from brochure, "Talking about Domestic Violence with Engaged Couples – A Guide for Pastors" (Cleveland: Catholic Diocese of Cleveland, Dept. for Marriage and Family Ministry, www.clevelandcatholiccharities.org/mfm). Used with permission.

16. See Carol J. Adams, *Woman Battering* (Minneapolis: Fortress Press, 1994), p. 39–42, for excellent information related to this process.

17. Thanks to Mark D. Houglum, M.Div, Ph.D. (Presbyterian Counseling

NOTES

Service, Seattle, WA) for exploring this aspect of premarital counseling with me.

18. Isaiah 61:1, adapted from the United Church of Christ *Book of Worship* (NY: United Church of Christ Office for Church Life and Leadership, 1986), p. 406.

Chapter Six

19. For a more thorough discussion of issues and strategies raised in this chapter, see Carol J. Adams, *Woman Battering* (Minneapolis: Fortress Press, 1994).

20. Information here and on the following page is adapted from *National Consensus Guidelines on Identifying and Responding to Domestic Violence Victimization in Health Care Settings* (San Francisco: Family Violence Prevention Fund, Sept. 2002), p. 14–16. (http://endabuse.org, 415/252-8900, TTY 800/595-4889).

21. Rev. Dr. Anne Marie Hunter, Exec. Dir., Safe Havens Interfaith Partnership Against Domestic Violence, Boston, MA. Personal communication, 2005. Used with permission.

22. Some of the material in this section is adapted from the excellent discussion of these issues in Carol J. Adams, *Woman Battering* (Minneapolis: Fortress Press, 1994).

Chapter Seven

23. Adapted by author from Eugene H. Peterson, *The Message Remix: The Bible in Contemporary Language* (Colorado Springs: NavPress, 2003).

SELECTED RESOURCES

BOOKS

Theological/Pastoral Guidance

Adams, Carol J. *Woman Battering* (Creative Pastoral Care and Counseling Series). Minneapolis: Fortress Press, 1994.

Adams, Carol J., & Marie M. Fortune (eds.). *Violence Against Women and Children – A Christian Theological Sourcebook.* New York: Continuum Publ. Co., 1995.

Cooper-White, Pamela. *The Cry of Tamar – Violence Against Women and the Church's Response.* Minneapolis: Fortress Press, 1995.

Fortune, Marie M. *Keeping the Faith: Guidance for Christian Women Facing Abuse.* San Francisco: Harper San Francisco, 1987.

Fortune, Marie M. *Violence in the Family: A Curriculum for Clergy and Other Helpers.* Cleveland: Pilgrim Press, 1991.

Gottman, John M. *When Men Batter Women.* New York: Simon and Schuster, 1998.

Livingston, David J. *Healing Violent Men: A Model for Christian Communities.* Minneapolis: Fortress Press, 2002.

Miles, Rev. Al. *Domestic Violence – What Every Pastor Needs to Know.* Minneapolis: Fortress Press, 2000.

Murphy, Nancy A. *God's Reconciling Love: A Pastor's Handbook on Domestic Violence.* Seattle: FaithTrust Institute, 2003.

Poling, James Newton, & Christie Cozad Neuger (eds.). *Men's Work in Preventing Violence Against Women.* Binghamton, NY: Haworth Pastoral Press, 2002.

Poling, James N. *Understanding Male Violence: Pastoral Care Issues.* St Louis, MO: Chalice Press, 2003.

West, Traci C. *Wounds of the Spirit: Black Women, Violence, and Resistance Ethics.* New York: NYU Press, 1999.

Marriage Preparation and Enrichment

Gottman, John M., & Nan Silver. *The Seven Principles for Making Marriage Work.* New York: Three Rivers Press, 1999.

Gottman, John M., & Nan Silver. *The Relationship Cure.* New York: Three Rivers Press, 2001.

Luther, Donald J. (ed.). *Preparing for Marriage.* Minneapolis, MN: Fortress Press, 1992.

Midgley, John M.V., & Susan Vollmer Midgley. *A Decision to Love.* Mystic CT: Twenty-Third Publications, 1998.

Parrott, Les & Leslie Parrott. *Saving Your Marriage Before It Starts.* Grand Rapids, MI: Zondervan, 1995.

Wood, Norma S., & Lisa M. Leber. *Now Bring Your Joy to This Wedding – Couples in Premarital Preparation.* Lima, OH: CSS Publ. Co., 2002.

VIDEOS

From FaithTrust Institute
Seattle, Washington
www.faithtrustinstitute.org

Broken Vows: Religious Perspectives on Domestic Violence (video & facilitator's guide). 1994.

Wings Like a Dove: Healing for the Abused Christian Woman (video & facilitator's guide). 1997.

Love—All That and More: A Video Series and Curriculum on Healthy Relationships (3 videos & facilitator's guides). 2000.

Domestic Violence: What Churches Can Do (video & facilitator's guide). 2002.

Pastoral Care for Domestic Violence: Case Studies for Clergy (video & trainer's manual). Spring 2006.

INTERNET RESOURCES

Faith-Based Programs Dealing with Domestic Violence

FaithTrust Institute
Seattle, WA
www.faithtrustinstitute.org
FaithTrust Institute is an international, multifaith organization working to end sexual and domestic violence. They offer a wide range of services and resources, including training, consultation, and educational materials to provide communities and advocates with the tools and knowledge they need to address the religious and cultural issues related to abuse. FaithTrust Institute works with many communities, including Asian and Pacific Islander, Buddhist, Jewish, Latino/a, Muslim, Black, Anglo, Indigenous, Protestant, and Roman Catholic.

Sabbath of Domestic Peace: An Interfaith Coalition
Philadelphia, PA
www.sabbathofdomesticpeace.org
This organization is an interdisciplinary, interfaith coalition to encourage and support the involvement of religious leaders and congregations in the greater Philadelphia area in their efforts to prevent and reduce domestic violence by raising awareness and providing educational and resource materials, information, educational programs, and liturgical resources.

Safe Havens Interfaith Partnership Against Domestic Violence
Boston, MA
www.interfaithpartners.org
Safe Havens is an inter-religious nonprofit dedicated to ending domestic violence by working with faith-based organizations to create systemic community change through educational and advocacy initiatives. Safe Havens' approach to domestic violence intervention and prevention work prioritizes the safety of victims and accountability of batterers over any religious, political or financial interests.

Because domestic violence cuts across all boundaries of religion, age, race, ethnicity, class, gender, and geography, Safe Havens is committed to working with diverse communities.

Definitions & Statistics on Domestic Violence

National Center for Injury Prevention and Control
Centers for Disease Control and Prevention
Atlanta, GA
www.cdc.gov/ncipc/factsheets/ipvfacts.htm
Intimate Partner Violence: Fact Sheet – This site has collected a vast array of statistics, information, and resources.

Canadian National Clearinghouse on Family Violence (NCFV)
Ottawa, Ontario
www.phac-aspc.gc.ca/ncfv-cnivf/familyviolence/index.html
The NCFV is Canada's resource centre for information on violence within relationships of kinship, intimacy, dependency or trust.

*Secular Programs & Organizations Committed
to Prevention of Domestic Violence*

Oakland County Coordinating Council Against Domestic Violence
Bloomfield Hills, MI
www.domesticviolence.org/define.html
This site is a Domestic Violence Handbook and offers a thorough index of information resources. It is an example of a secular, local resource center.

Men Ending Violence
Richmond, VA
www.vahealth.org/civp/sexualviolence/menendingviolence/index.html
This website focuses on involving men in the reduction of sexual violence through education, training, funding, and resources. This web page is a part of the Virginia Department of Health's Sexual Violence Prevention Program.

SELECTED RESOURCES

National Coalition Against Domestic Violence (NCADV)
Denver, CO
www.ncadv.org
The Mission of the NCADV is to organize for collective power by advancing transformative work, thinking and leadership of communities and individuals working to end violence. Their list of links to other domestic violence websites is quite extensive.

Family Violence Prevention Fund (FVPF), San Francisco, CA
www.endabuse.org
For more than two decades, the FVPF has worked to end violence against women and children around the world. Instrumental in developing the landmark Violence Against Women Act passed by Congress in 1994, the FVPF has continued to break new ground by reaching new audiences including men and youth, promoting leadership within communities to ensure that violence prevention efforts become self-sustaining, and transforming the way health care providers, police, judges, employers, and others address violence.

Hotline Information

National Domestic Violence Hotline (NDVH)
A project of the Texas Council on Family Violence
www.ndvh.org/ 800-799-7233 800-787-3224 (TTY)
The NDVH serves as the only center in the nation that provides information regarding 5000 local and nationwide shelters and service providers available for victims, friends and family who often call for life saving help. The Hotline operates 24 hours a day in more than 140 languages, with a TTY line available for the deaf.

HANDOUTS

HANDOUTS FOR USE BY PASTORS

There are many printed resources for pastors to use in the context of premarital counseling; you will find a list of some of these in the resource section of this book. They may be adapted for your own purposes in premarital counseling; it is important to check copyright guidelines before using.

Included here are a number of copy-ready handouts for pastoral use. Some have suggestions for when and how to use the handout; others are self evident. You may adapt these for use in your own premarital counseling.

They include:

1. Covenant Circles of Support..........................72
2. Covenantal Communications........................74
3. What Every Couple Needs to Know.................76
4. Power and Control Wheel..........................78
5. Equality Wheel..................................80
6. What Ties or Severs the Covenant 82
7. Contrasting Contractual and Covenantal Relationships.........84
8. Constructive and Destructive Ways of Dealing with Anger 86
9. What Does a Trusting Relationship Look Like? 88

COVENANT CIRCLES OF SUPPORT

Use this worksheet to remember those who surround you with encouragement.

As you consider your marriage journey ahead, think about persons you want in your lives who will offer support for your marital health and companionship – in good as well as challenging times. They might be people who will bring out your best as marriage partners and who will be there to help in times of difficulty. Decide together, and then write their names somewhere in the space for each circle of support.

    A. Closest family and friends we see from time to time.

    B. Other person or couples we'd like as companions for our marital journey.

    C. Counselors, church, community resources that offer support and wisdom.

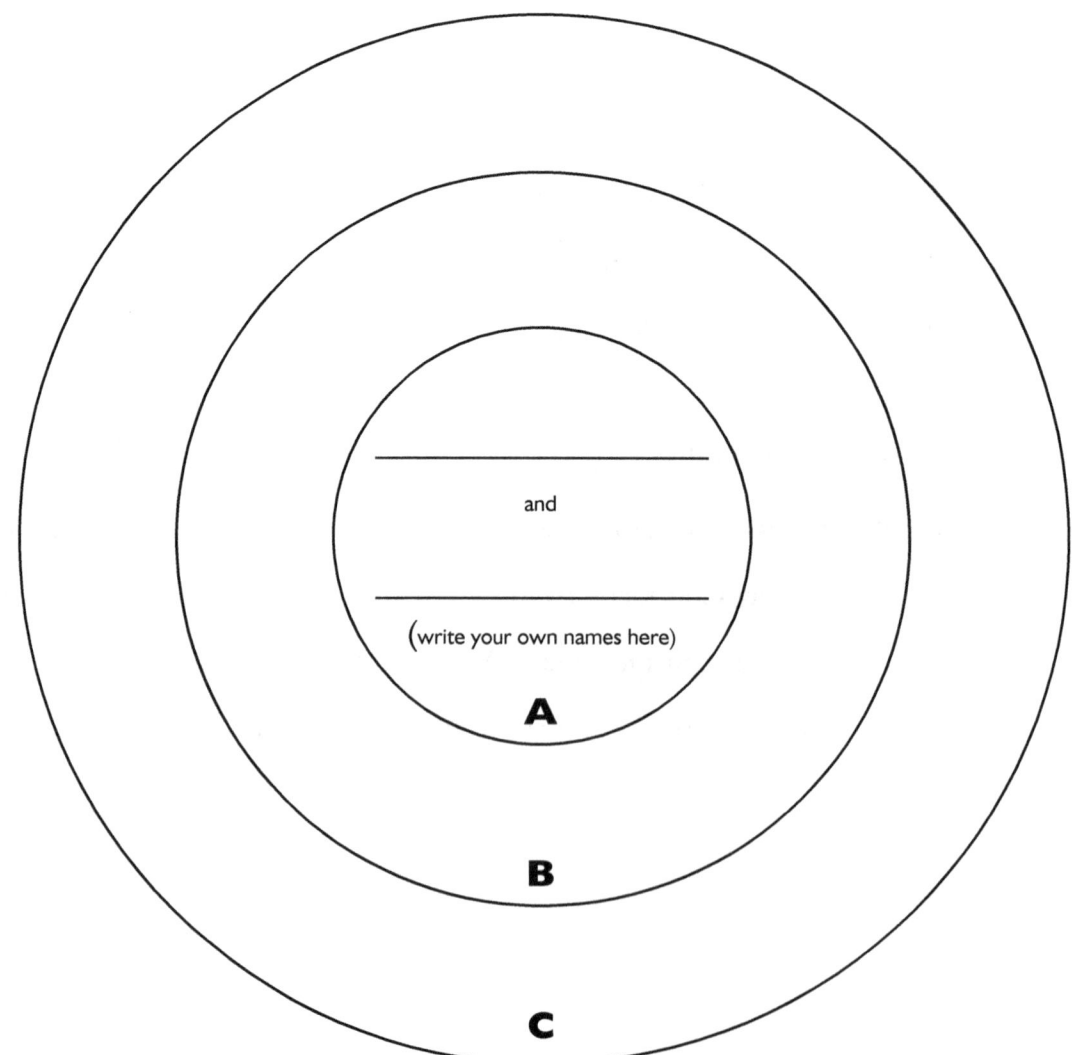

© 2006 Susan Yarrow Morris. Used with permission.

Opening The Door | 72

COPY OPPOSITE PAGE
FOR DISTRIBUTION

COVENANT CIRCLES OF SUPPORT
HANDOUT USE NOTES

Context within which to use handout…

This is an opportunity to remind couples that they are not alone on their marital journeys. There are times when others can both encourage and celebrate their covenant life together.

Suggested use:

- At the close of premarital counseling sessions.
- Encourage partners to think of other persons who may be appropriately named for each of these categories.

Questions to stimulate discussion…

Closest family and friends:

- Who are those persons/couples whom you see as models of healthy covenant partnerships?
- Who are persons who help you celebrate life, with whom you may share relaxed activities, parenting wisdom, or festive meals?

Other persons/couples not as well known or seen as often:

- Who are those persons whom you trust to be there for you in all times?
- Who are persons who remind you that God's love is at the heart of your loving partnership?

Counselors, church, community:

- Who are those professional persons to whom you would turn if you couldn't work through a difficult conflict or needed support?
- Who are persons in your faith community with whom you worship and celebrate life, and who you feel make the world a better place?

ELEMENTS OF COVENANT PARTNER COMMUNICATION

Why is this kind of communication important?

- Because partners need to stay closely in touch to sustain and deepen covenant life.
- Because words and actions are tangible expressions of mutual love, respect, care and trust between partners.

What skills are needed to communicate this way?

1. A capacity to reflect on one's own behaviors

   a. What do I communicate with my tone of voice?

   b. What does my body language (eyes, posture, facial expression) communicate?

   c. Do my words and actions communicate the same thing?

   d. Is my partner – or are others – ever uncomfortable when I speak or act?

2. A capacity to listen covenantally rather than adversarially

Covenantal Listening	_Adversarial Listening_
Seeking to understand the other	**Defending one's view**
Empathy – feeling what the other is feeling	Protecting one's turf
Dialogical – speaking back & forth to clarify	**A win-lose debate tone**
Offering time for partner to speak	Interrupting, interpreting
Focus is on partner	**Focus is on self**

3. A capacity to speak truthfully in love…not speak "THE TRUTH"!

   - DESCRIBE what YOU are feeling, thinking, seeing, hoping, dreaming, confused about, asking, etc.
   - DO NOT discount, accuse, generalize, change the topic, argue, wander, lecture, moralize, give advice, make fun of, or keep quiet!

THE MORE COVENANT PARTNERS PRACTICE THESE SKILLS, THE MORE A CLIMATE OF TRUST AND SAFETY IS CREATED WHERE LOVE CAN FLOURISH.

© 2006 Susan Yarrow Morris. Used with permission.

COPY OPPOSITE PAGE
FOR DISTRIBUTION

ELEMENTS OF COVENANT PARTNER COMMUNICATION

HANDOUT USE NOTES

Context within which to use handout…

This handout is best used by a pastor or counselor as a worksheet with a couple. Walking through each of the points and inviting role plays or practice of specific skills is encouraged. The topics included here can best come to life as the exercises invite partners to discuss, practice and explore these dynamics in their relationships, past and present.

Questions to stimulate discussion…

Their capacity to reflect:

- When does each of you find yourself most able to reflect on your own behavior and its impact on others?
- How do you respond when you sense others are uncomfortable with something you said or did?

Their capacity to listen:

- Who, in your family or friendship circles, models these two contrasting listening postures? What do you admire or find difficult in each? How do you feel in the presence of each?
- When is it easy for each of you to listen covenantally? When not?

Their capacity to speak truthfully:

- What is it like when you talk together truthfully?
- In your experience, what results from not speaking truthfully?
- Can you talk about a time when speaking truthfully made a difference for the better?
- Can you think of a time when you believed you had "the Truth?" What was your partner's response?

And final question:

- What three dimensions of covenantal communication will you be working on as you begin your marriage?

Opening The Door | 75

WHAT EVERY COUPLE NEEDS TO KNOW...

We care very much about the health and joy of your marriage. The well-being of each of you as covenant partners in life is vital. For that reason, we share this information with you.

What is DOMESTIC VIOLENCE?

A pattern of assaultive and coercive behaviors -

It can be experienced as: *physical   sexual   emotional   economic.*

Adults or adolescents use it against their intimate partners.

DOMESTIC VIOLENCE may include these behaviors:

hitting   name-calling   slapping   use of weapons   pushing   kicking

forced sex   threats of violence   attacks against property or pets

humiliation   extreme jealousy   controlling partner's social life or money

DOMESTIC VIOLENCE occurs in couples from all socioeconomic classes, ethnic groups and faith traditions.

- Nearly one out of three women in the U.S. experiences at least one physical assault by a partner in her adulthood (American Psychological Association, 1996).[1]
- A woman is physically abused by her husband every 9 seconds in the U.S. (The Sabbath of Domestic Peace 2004)[2]

When alcohol or drugs are used, DOMESTIC VIOLENCE is likely to increase in severity and frequency.

If you have experienced any of these behaviors...or are afraid that you might...or if you have done these behaviors...or wanted to do them,

We encourage you to seek help and support — you are not alone...we care.

Local Domestic Violence info number: _____

National Domestic Violence hotline number: 1-800-799-SAFE   1-800 787-3224 TTY

Local batterer's intervention program: _____

Your pastor's name and phone number: _____

---

[1] Quoted in SaraKay Smullens, "Counseling the Clergy on How to Help Victims of Domestic Violence," *Annals of the American Psychotherapy Association*, Nov/Dec. 2001

[2] From "Responding to Domestic Violence: Making Changes, Bringing Hope," a publication of the Sabbath of Domestic Peace, Philadelphia, PA, 2001, www.sabbathofdomesticpeace.org

© 2006 Susan Yarrow Morris. Used with permission.

COPY OPPOSITE PAGE
FOR DISTRIBUTION

WHAT EVERY COUPLE NEEDS TO KNOW…
HANDOUT USE NOTES

Context within which to use handout…

(See page 35 for an explanation of how and when this handout might best be used.)

You can supplement this page with the two following handouts:

- Power and Control Wheel
- Equality Wheel

The two wheels provide additional examples to illustrate the contrasts between abusive and non-abusive relationships. Each segment corresponds in the two wheels. It is good to insure that each partner in the couple understands the difference between unequal and shared power and control in their relationship. By providing the safe, conversational space to explore these distinctions, clear guidelines can be acknowledged for acceptable vs. unacceptable behavior. This may be the first time the partners have had an opportunity to think about and explore these critical dynamics.

POWER AND CONTROL WHEEL

Are you in an Abusive Relationship?

Domestic Abuse Intervention Project
202 E. Superior St. Duluth, MN 55802
218-722-2781

POWER AND CONTROL WHEEL
HANDOUT USE NOTES

Context within which to use handout…

This handout can be used to illustrate the points raised in the previous handout: "What Every Couple Needs to Know."

It is designed to be contrasted to the following handout: "Equality Wheel."

EQUALITY WHEEL

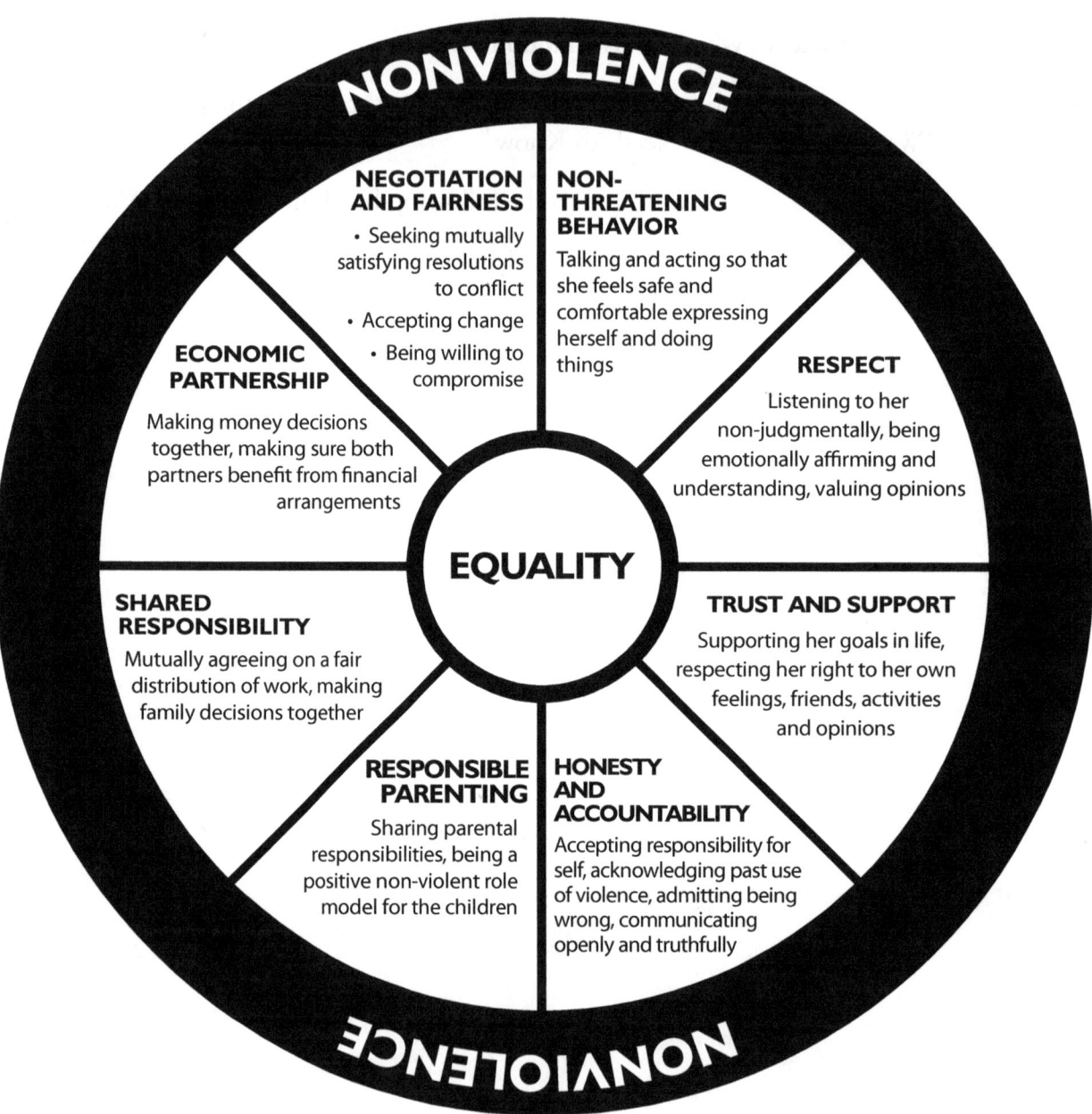

Domestic Abuse Intervention Project
202 E. Superior St. Duluth, MN 55802
218-722-2781

EQUALITY WHEEL

HANDOUT USE NOTES

Context within which to use handout…

This handout can be used to contrast the points raised in the handout, "What Every Couple Needs to Know."

It is designed to show the alternatives to the power abuses set forth in the handout, "Power and Control Wheel." It is an opportunity to be sure the couple understands this contrast and sees the many ways a couple can relate within the context of a covenantal relationship.

Questions to stimulate discussion…

Using this wheel as a form of appreciation

- Which of these behaviors does each of you regularly practice?
- What is a recent example in your lives for each of these behaviors?
- How can you acknowledge the importance of equality in your relationship?

Using this wheel as a goal setting structure

- Which of these behaviors do you want to improve?
- Where are specific opportunities in your relationship to practice each behavior?
- How could this wheel become a tool for improving the quality of your relationship?

WHAT **TIES** OR **SEVERS** THE COVENANT

What "ties" marital connection

- Mutual love and respect
- Honoring vows and promises
- Open-ended anticipation of abundant shared life
- Sustained, hopeful sense that the commitment is forever
- Daily experience that the relationship is life-giving
- Responsibility for faithful words and actions

What "severs" marital connection

- Emotional, physical or sexual abuse
- Broken promises, dishonesty, secrecy
- Conditional, limited emotional commitment
- Sense of relational fragility
- Fear of a tenuous future and what's ahead
- Daily experience that trust is eroded
- Lack of mutual accountability

© 2006 Susan Yarrow Morris. Used with permission.

COPY OPPOSITE PAGE
FOR DISTRIBUTION

WHAT **TIES** OR **SEVERS** THE COVENANT
HANDOUT USE NOTES

Context within which to use handout…

Encourage couples to add their own specific elements of what "Ties" and "Severs" to the starter list provided on this handout. Doing so personalizes the list and empowers each partner to name those elements that strengthen or weaken the sense of covenantal connection.

Another option would be to invite couples to review their friends' and families' relationships for examples of each of the elements listed under "Ties" or "Severs." Hopefully this will facilitate coming to a common understanding of these two lists.

Questions to stimulate discussion…

Generating a couple's own list

- What is missing from the list of elements that tie that is true in your relationship and needs to be added to make this list your own?
- What is missing from the list of elements that sever that is true in your relationship and needs to be added to make this list your own?

Finding examples in others' relationships

- Where, in your circle of family and friends, do you find examples of each characteristic?
- What more can you learn regarding these two lists by thinking about other couples you know?

CONTRASTING CONTRACTUAL AND COVENANTAL RELATIONSHIPS[1]

Marriages based on mutual respect and love are **covenantal** relationships. This kind of relationship is rare and needs to be tended with care and ongoing commitment.

Because most relationships in our lives are **contractual,** we often do not have the skills necessary to sustain lively covenantal relationships. This is a way of looking at these two kinds of relationships in our lives.

CONTRACT (Latin: *contrahere*)

Contract means to draw together, to restrict, to diminish, to limit. It is used with things, property or personal belongings. When persons are involved, it is not the *person* who is hired or contracted for, but the *services* to be provided. Contracts are ended by mutual agreement, by failure to live up to the terms, or by civil intervention.

Contracts, in summary:	**Contracts** deal with:
<ul><li>Draw together</li><li>Restrict</li><li>Diminish</li><li>Limit</li><li>Specific and time limited</li><li>Drawn on basis of need</li><li>Assume everything is settled</li></ul>	<ul><li>Things, ideas, services</li><li>Personal belongings, property</li></ul> **Contracts** are ended by: <ul><li>Agreement</li><li>Failure to live up to terms</li><li>Legal and specified consequences</li></ul>

COVENANT (Latin: *foedus*)

Covenant is an expansive and all-embracing relationship. The root word (fidus) means to trust, to have faith in, to entrust oneself to another; thus, covenant is a relationship of mutual trust and fidelity. Covenants end by violation of this promise, or a breach of faith on the part of either or both of the partners.

Covenants, in summary, are:	**Covenants** deal with
<ul><li>Based on faith in another</li><li>Entrusting oneself to other</li><li>All embracing and expansive</li><li>Open-ended but assume permanence</li><li>Are re-chosen again and again</li><li>Made on the basis of shared life and dreams</li><li>Assume everything is unsettled</li></ul>	<ul><li>Persons, promises mutuality, fidelity</li><li>Intertwining of lives</li></ul> **Covenants** are ended by <ul><li>Breach of faith by either partner</li><li>Violation acknowledged by offender</li><li>No guarantee of forgiveness or reconciliation</li></ul>

---

[1] Several of the ideas in this handout were adapted from "Christian Marriage: Contract or Covenant?", Paul F. Palmer, S.J., *Theological Studies*, Volume 33 (Format: Serial), 1972, pp. 617-65.

COPY OPPOSITE PAGE
FOR DISTRIBUTION

CONTRASTING CONTRACTUAL AND COVENANTAL RELATIONSHIPS

HANDOUT USE NOTES

Context within which to use handout…

Much of the "business" of getting married is about contracting for services – from wedding coordinator to photographer to reception location – and so on. Even the marriage license is a contract with the state. Yet from the pastoral perspective, the most important commitment being celebrated in the marriage ceremony is much more profound than any of these attention-demanding and energy-absorbing arrangements. It is ironic that all these preoccupations give plentiful opportunities to ignore the critical questions about the quality of the life-long spiritual journey on which the couple is about to embark. This handout sets forth some distinctions, inviting the couple to consider the unique nature of their vows in a world that primarily negotiates life through contracts.

Suggestions for pastoral use:

- When speaking with engaged couples in premarital counseling, it is helpful to contrast these two kinds of relationships by using real-life examples.

- Exploring typical contractual relationships in our lives (e.g., store clerk, teacher, physician, etc.) and covenantal relationships in our lives (family, some friendships, church membership, and marital partners) affirms the unique significance of the marriage relationship and the serious nature of its responsibilities.

Questions to stimulate discussion…

1. How is your relationship with your house painter different from your relationship with your spouse?
2. What are your responsibilities to your house painter (plumber, doctor, etc.)? How is s/he held accountable?
3. What are your responsibilities to your marriage partner? How is each of you held accountable?
4. How will your marriage vows inspire you to be a responsible covenant partner?

CONSTRUCTIVE AND DESTRUCTIVE WAYS OF DEALING WITH ANGER

CONSTRUCTIVE behaviors and attitudes

It is never right to threaten or abuse my partner, physically or emotionally, no matter how angry I am.

When I'm angry, I know it.

Feeling angry is a normal human emotion.

When I am angry with my partner, we talk it over.

I can control how I express my anger.

When I'm angry with someone else, I don't take it out on my partner.

Even when I'm angry with my partner, I do not put him/her down.

When my partner is angry with me, I try to listen without becoming defensive.

When my feelings are hurt, I want to talk about it.

When my partner is angry, I help him/her talk about the issues which concern him or her.

I am satisfied that my partner and I can express anger appropriately and that we understand it is a part of a mature relationship.

DESTRUCTIVE behaviors and attitudes

Physical and verbal abuses are natural ways to express my anger.

When I am angry, I say critical things to my partner.

I'm not even aware when I am angry.

Anger is wrong; I shouldn't be angry.

When my partner expresses her/his anger, I tend to become angry.

I keep anger inside until I explode.

When my feelings are hurt, I tend to pout or sulk.

If my partner and I are angry with each other, our marriage is falling apart.

Expressing anger is scary for me.

COPY OPPOSITE PAGE
FOR DISTRIBUTION

CONSTRUCTIVE AND DESTRUCTIVE WAYS OF DEALING WITH ANGER

HANDOUT USE NOTES

Context within which to use handout…

One way to use this handout is to ask each partner, in turn, to

- read each line;
- decide if it is truly what he or she believes; and
- comment on his or her perspective.

It is likely that there will be many responses of "of course" and "for sure" while moving through the "CONSTRUCTIVE" list. However, there may be differences of opinion when one partner says a particular statement isn't really all that important and isn't true for her/him. For example, "I can control how I express my anger" might result in the comment, "I believe it is important to be honest and just vent my anger, so we can get on with fixing what's wrong." At a time like this, facilitate a conversation about what is constructive and what is destructive in this behavior and attitude in general, and then bring it back to the couple. The important thing is that the partners agree about what is constructive or destructive for them in their experience.

When you reach the "DESTRUCTIVE" list, there might be an added charge in the air due to the negative implication of the heading. Partners may feel defensive if they admit to owning one on the list. Having each partner say the words of the statement, think about whether s/he believes it is true or not, and then inviting the other partner's perspective, can clear the air and create common understanding. Your role as facilitator is critical in keeping this whole process part of deepening the partners' mutual understanding and making it acceptable to discuss these things.

WHAT DOES A TRUSTING RELATIONSHIP LOOK LIKE?

A trusting relationship of covenantal love creates a safe place for body, mind and soul for both partners. It provides a sense of trust, security, and mutual kindness in difficult times. It counts on responsible, direct and mature communication, rather than demeaning or disrespectful communication or game-playing.

These questions might help you, as covenant partners, create a safer place for each other.

1. **Risk taking:** Can I tell you what I think and feel with some assurance that you will not laugh at me, put me down, tell me that I shouldn't feel this way or reject me for my thoughts and feelings, whatever they may be? Do I encourage your risk-taking in the same way?

2. **Understanding:** Do you genuinely try to understand how I think and feel and believe? Do I have some assurance that you will understand what I am feeling/thinking/believing without necessarily agreeing with me? Do I try to understand you with similar respect?

3. **Empathy:** Are you "sympatico" with me? Do you affirm that my feelings are real and do you take them seriously? Do I try to do the same with your feelings?

4. **Right to be different:** Will you allow me to be different from you, to have some different interests and friends, to explore and grow in ways I think are important? Do I offer you the same freedom?

5. **Explicitness, Honesty:** Are you open and direct when sharing ideas or feelings with me? Do I feel I can be candid with you?

6. **Making changes:** Can you help me assess a situation and decide on a new course of action (if I choose to do so) or can we comfortably work together to make changes which affect us both? Am I able to help you in a similar way?

7. **Dependability:** Can I count on you to say what you mean and mean what you say? Can I rely on you to nurture the trusting relationship we have? Am I a reliable partner – to be counted upon to do my best in the same way?

8. **Respect:** Am I safe from the shame of being put down, belittled, embarrassed, and dismissed? Do my words and behaviors always reflect respect for you?

When these dynamics are not present, or when fear of expressing and being yourself is present, trust is eroded and the covenant can be at risk.

(adapted from Morris Titkin, M.D.)

WHAT DOES A TRUSTING RELATIONSHIP LOOK LIKE?
HANDOUT USE NOTES

Context within which to use handout…

At its core, a covenantal relationship is dependent upon mutual trust and faithfulness. This handout encourages a couple to ask basic questions about significant aspects of a vibrant, trusting bond.

One way to use these questions would be to have each partner give a value as to how applicable these attributes are in their relationship (0 = rarely; 10 = almost always). After each has completed his/her assessment, facilitate a discussion about those attributes they feel really good about. Acknowledge them for the strength this represents in their lives together.

Then gently move to those attributes which one or both partners report experiencing rarely. The discussion is best directed towards how they might increase the frequency of behaviors and attitudes suggested by the specific attribute, rather than debating past deficiencies. Often there is an example of broken trust in the past that triggers a low evaluation for one or both partners. Step firmly into understanding the episode and then guide the couple in brainstorming ways to provide healthier alternatives in the present and future. Help them move to a specific set of proactive commitments that will move their attribute evaluation up the scale towards a ten in the days ahead.

Throughout the process of using this handout, the goal is both educational and evaluative. Ask the couple "What is missing on this list that you two want to add to enhance your covenantal, trusting relationship?" Help them find the balance between their idealistic expectations and a realistic assessment of trust building/sustaining skills.

APPENDICES

LIST OF APPENDICES

1. "Saving the Family: When is Covenant Broken?" by Mitzi N. Eilts . . .93
2. Additional Statistics on Domestic Violence 101
3. Predictors of Domestic Violence 103
4. Indicators that a Man May Kill His Partner 105
5. Accountability - "A man who has battered a woman becomes accountable when…" 107
6. Resources Commonly Used in Premarital Counseling 109
7. "Counseling the Clergy on How to Help Victims of Domestic Violence" 115
8. Responding to Domestic Violence: Guidelines for Clergy 119
9. "A Community Checklist" for Religious Communities 123

APPENDIX 1

APPENDIX 1
SAVING THE FAMILY: WHEN IS COVENANT BROKEN?*

Mitzi N. Eilts

For those of us in the church, there are critical questions presented by the reality of domestic violence. Is maintaining the family unit more sacred than the well-being and safety of the individuals within it? Is there any spiritual reason for suffering or abuse to be endured which is perpetrated by one member of the family against another? Who is responsible for breaking up the family –the one who leaves home and partner or parent to escape the abuse or the one who is being abusive?

To find some answers to these questions requires that we reexamine what constitutes family in our faith traditions. What is the nature of the covenant around which we build family? What are the principles of covenant as established by God on which we pattern our covenants with each other? Is there any evidence or precedent in scripture or our faith traditions for the breaking of covenant? What are they? Is the only kind of family "to be saved" the nuclear family with father *and* mother and children? In this chapter these questions are examined so that the religious community and service providers might consider what a danger it is to apply a save-the-family ethic without equal consideration of other spiritual ethics and values.

Covenant Making

Covenant making is older than the Judeo-Christian tradition; there is evidence of this in the language used in the Old Testament that comes from treaty-making language of the nations and tribes occupying the territory into which the Israelites moved.[1] Covenant making is the establishment of an agreement between two parties defining the relationship (responsibilities and obligations)

---

* From *Violence Against Women and Children: A Christian Theological Sourcebook*, Carol J. Adams and Marie M. Fortune, Editors (New York: The Continuum Publishers, 1995), p 440-450. Used with permission.

between them. It may be an agreement between equals (mutual, parity) or a unilateral agreement (suzerainty) in which one party must accept the conditions presented by the other due to favors owed or difference in power.

It is generally understood and accepted in the Jewish and Christian traditions that covenants with God are initiated by God. There is nevertheless some recognition of mutuality in God's covenant making with us in that God takes on promises and responsibilities to uphold as well as naming obligations to be upheld by those to whom the covenant is offered. (In other words, covenants are good for us *and* good for God.) A common thread in all of God's covenants is a promise of deliverance and well-being, liberation from suffering, persecution, or oppression (either already bestowed, to come, or to be continued), and in exchange God seeks loyalty and commitment---commitment of heart reflected in behavior.

Consider the covenants established with Noah (Gen. 9:1: out of chaos a promise never again to destroy the earth); with Abraham and Sarah (Gen.17:1: out of barrenness the promise of generations to carry on); with Moses (out of bondage a promise of a home). Covenants made with the God of the Hebrew Scriptures and the Christian Testament have as their most basic element the offer of liberation from bondage or affliction—the offer of new life, life as God intended it to be for us.[2]

> For I the Lord love justice, I hate robbery and wrong; I will faithfully give them their recompense, and I will make an everlasting covenant with them. (Isa. 61:8)

> I call heaven and earth to witness against you this day, that I have set before you life and death, blessing and curse; therefore choose life, that you and your descendants may live. (Deut. 30:19)

> I came that they may have life and have it more abundantly. (John 10:10)

We should remember that as the people of God we are in a constant process of renewing and reestablishing the covenant between God and ourselves. It is common to speak and act as though God's covenant with us is a settled event. Yet the covenant with Moses was offered anew to the Hebrew people through Joshua as they entered the promised land. The original covenant with Moses was a revision of the ones made with Noah and Abraham and Sarah, then renewed with Jacob. The Davidic covenant was seen as new, yet it was related to the one made with Abraham and Sarah. Jeremiah and the New Testament

---

[1] For more detail on treaty language and form see George E. Mendenhall, "Covenant Form in Israelite Tradition," *The Biblical Archaeologist Reader*, 3rd ed., ed. E.F. Campbell, Jr. and D.N. Freedman (Garden City, N.Y., Doubleday, 1970).

[2] All scripture quotations are from the Revised Standard Version.

APPENDIX 1

authors represented the covenant as being reestablished in new ways. Renewal of covenant has been seen as necessary and has been practiced as new generations have emerged with different conditions in their lives, so that all covenants are relevant to the present circumstances.[3]

> Behold, the days are coming, says the Lord, when I will make a new covenant with the house of Israel and the house of Judah, not like the covenant which I made with their fathers when I took them by the hand to bring them out of the land of Egypt, my covenant which they broke....But this is the covenant which I will make with the house of Israel after those days, says the Lord: I will put my law within them and I will write it upon their hearts; and I will be their God, and they shall be my people. (Jer.31:31-33)

> Blessed be the Lord God of Israel, for God has visited and redeemed his people, and has raised up a horn of salvation for us in the house of his servant David....that we should be saved from our enemies, and from the hand of all who hate us; to perform the mercy promised to our ancestors, and to remember his holy covenant, the oath which God swore to our father Abraham, to grant that we, being delivered from the hand of our enemies might serve God without fear. (Luke 1:68-69, 71-73)

Consequences of Covenant Breaking

Additionally, there is history of covenants being broken between God and God's people. The language of God's covenants acknowledges this possibility by the use of blessings and curses.

> [BLESSINGS] If you walk in my statutes and observe my commandments and do them, then I will give you your rains in their season and the land shall yield its increase, and the trees of the field shall yield their fruit....And I will give you peace in the land, and you shall lie down and none shall make you afraid;....And I will have regard for you and make you fruitful and multiply you, and will confirm my covenant with you....And I will walk among you and will be your god and you shall be my people.

> [CURSES] But if you will not hearken to me, and will not do all these commandments, if you spurn my statutes, and if your soul abhors my ordinances, so that you will not do all my commandments, but break my covenant; I will do this to you: I will appoint over you sudden terror,

---

[3] For further examples and discussion of covenant renewal see G.F. Mendenhall, "Covenant Forms in Israelite Tradition," in Old Testament Theology, Vol. 1, ed. Gerhard von Rad (New York: Harper & Row, 1962), 38.

consumption, and fever that waste the eyes and cause life to pine away…and
I will break the pride of your power. (Leviticus 26; see also Psalm 78 and
Deuteronomy 29)

These verses illustrate that there are consequences for the breaking of covenant—not so much wrath or vengeance, but the consequences of living life without God. For once we have broken the covenant(s) we make with God, we are in essence living in a world devoid of God and God's ways. Though it has become clear over time that God has an unending ability and desire to forgive our unfaithfulness or breaking of covenant, it has also remained true that there are consequences when we desert the ways of God. Change and amends (repentance) are necessary to restore covenant relationships.

And when all these things come upon you, the blessing and the curse, which I have set before you, and you call them to mind among all the nations where the Lord your God has driven you, and return to the Lord your God, you and your children, and obey his voice in all that I command you this day, with all your heart and all your soul; then the Lord your God will restore your fortunes and have compassion upon you, and will gather you again from all peoples where the Lord your God has scattered you. (Deut. 30:1-3)

Who Decides When a Covenant Is Broken?

When a covenant is broken, who names the fact? Is it the covenant breaker, the one who has ignored, forgotten, transgressed the promise made? Or is it the one who is still living by the promises, the one who is attempting to keep covenant? Again and again, throughout the scriptures, it is God or one called by God (prophets such as Jeremiah, Isaiah, and John the Baptist) who calls attention to the fact that the covenant has been broken. It is God who says "if you want to be in a relationship with me you must change your ways –return to the promises you made with me." God, the one who has been faithful, is the one who says the covenant is broken; the covenant no longer stands. It is the one who is faithful to the covenant who calls attention to the fact it has been broken, and *that* makes common sense, does it not?

Covenant Making in Human Relationships

The idea of covenant between God and human beings was quickly picked up and applied to human relationships in the scripture. In the book of Genesis we find Abraham making covenant with Abimelech, and then Jacob and Laban

APPENDIX 1

using the idea and language of covenant with each other. Their oaths of loyalty and promises of peace are bound in the language of covenant.

Similarly, as people of faith, we have continued to apply the model of covenant with God to our human relationships. A prime example of this is our understanding of marriage as a form of covenant--making and keeping promises with God as an essential witness. Historically, marriage has sometimes been understood as a mutual covenant between two equal parties, and other times as a covenant of protection/caretaking by one person in exchange for nurturing/ obedience by the other. (Notice the parallel to the model of treaties – mutual/ parity and suzerainty.) Evidence supports the mutual marriage covenant as the one that most closely resembles and fulfills the purpose of God in covenant making. It is the mutual/parity form of relationship which establishes a way of relating and a setting for the promotion of health and well-being (physical, emotional, and spiritual), a setting within which life as God intended it to be for us might be nurtured and sustained.

Rev. Joy Bussert, in her book, *Battered Women: From a Theology of Suffering to a Theology of Empowerment* examines some theological premises that have been instrumental in making the marriage covenant one of suzerainty. Her thesis is that ideas such as mind-body dualism (debasing the very nature of femaleness) or that men have a right and a spiritual duty to chastise women, have distorted the nature of relationships between women and men, setting the stage for domestic violence to occur.[4] Friar Cherubino in the Rules of Marriage adhered to in the city of Sienna in the middle to late fifteenth century, for example, expressed a rationale used today by some abusers.

> When you see your wife commit an offense, don't rush at her with insults and violent blows; rather first correct the wrong lovingly…but if your wife is of a servile disposition and has a crude shifty spirit, so that pleasant words have no affect, scold her sharply, bully and terrify her. And if this still doesn't work…take up a stick and beat her soundly…for it is better to punish the body and correct the soul than to damage the soul and spare the body….You should beat her…only when she commits a serious wrong; for example, if she blasphemes God or a saint, if she mutters the devil's name, if she likes being at the window and lends ready ear to dishonest men, or if she has taken to bad habits or bad company, or commits some other wrong that is a mortal sin. Then readily beat her, not in rage but out of charity and concern for her

---

[4] For more in-depth discussion of these issues see Joy M.K. Bussert, *Battered Women: From a Theology of Suffering to an Ethic of Empowerment* (New York: Division for Mission in Northern America/Lutheran Church in America, 1986).

APPENDIX 1

soul, so that the beating will resound to your merit and good.[5]

Any covenant of marriage based on the protector/provider and obeyer/nurturer model lends itself too easily to the idea that a man ought to, even has a duty to, keep his woman in line, for his sake and hers.[6] In contrast, a marriage covenant based on mutual respect and responsibility expects both parties to work on and uphold their promises to love, cherish, and obey – the command of God, not of each other.

Rev. Marie Fortune has outlined the elements necessary to a marriage covenant based on mutuality; these elements make possible the fulfillment of God's intentions for us in the relationship and are parallel to those in the covenant between God and God's people.

1. It is made in the full knowledge of the relationship.

2. It involves a mutual giving of self to the other.

3. It is assumed to be lasting.

4. It values mutuality, respect, and equality between persons.[7]

Such marriage does not leave room for abuse. If and when abuse does occur, it is clear that promises and vows have been broken and the covenant (trust) has been breached.

When physical violence or emotional abuse occurs within a marriage relationship, the very intent of the covenant is being broken. When abuse is occurring, marriage becomes a setting of bondage and affliction rather than a setting for God's ways of compassion, justice, and love to be practiced and lived out.

Yet a woman victimized in an abusive domestic relationship feels serious ethical/spiritual dilemmas about the marriage covenant. She has made promises that are still important and meaningful to her. One of those is that the relationship will be a lasting one. To stay in the relationship means to suffer further abuse, but to leave (temporarily or permanently) makes her feel as if she is breaking her promise. Many women thus stay and suffer the abuse, precisely because they take their commitment seriously. Seldom does it occur to the victim of the abuse (at

---

[5] Cherubino de sienna, Regole *della Vita Matrimoniale*, cited in Bussert, 13-14, from O'Faolain and Martines, *Not in God's Image*, 177.

[6] See Bussert, *Battered Women*, chapters 1 and 4 for further discussion.

[7] Rev. Marie M. Fortune, "A Commentary on Religious Issues in Family Violence," in *Violence in the Family: A Workshop Curriculum for Clergy and Other Helpers* (Cleveland: Pilgrim Press, 1991), 137-51. Marie Fortune's writings and workshops have made immeasurable impact on my thinking as expressed in this chapter.

least in the beginning) – or to friends, family or the church – that the covenant has already been broken by the behavior of her partner.

Saving the Family

There is a big problem with the concept of saving the family (keeping covenant or the appearance of covenant) when it is applied indiscriminately to families in which domestic abuse/violence is present. The problem is that meaningless suffering and sometimes even death are very real consequences. The victim holds on for many reasons, one of which is usually hope – hope that what the marriage is supposed to be might be restored. It is common for the victim to persist in the hope that her patience will last longer than his abuse. Often this attitude is reinforced by church teachings on long suffering which may apply in settings where one is *choosing* to make a stand on behalf of God's ideals in this world, but which do not apply when the suffering is perpetrated by another who has promised to live according to God's ways with her.

In abusive families, hope and patience without safety for the victims and intervention for the abuser are dangerous because unless he takes responsibility for his actions and seeks help, the cycle of abuse will continue and worsen. Any chance that the covenant relationship might be restored requires both confession (taking responsibility for wrongdoing) and serious repentance on the part of the abuser, achieved by consistent participation in an abuser's program.

Victims often remain long past the danger point for some other emotional and religious reasons as well. Guilt is a common reason. The world around us reinforces the notion that the marriage relationship is primarily the responsibility of the woman. In many Jewish and Christian traditions women are told that marriage is the domain in which they are to live out their service to God. Therefore, if something is going wrong it must be their fault.

Most battered women have been told by at least one person that she must have done something to deserve such treatment. Most women hear that message from many sources, including their religious leaders and communities. Too seldom is the belief voiced that covenant is a two-way street, a partnership with responsibilities and obligations for both people involved. Too seldom is the one who is really breaking covenant, the abuser, being called to account for creating a home environment that is so oppressive that his partner needs to seek safety and peace elsewhere.

Victims/survivors often stay on in an abusive relationship for years because of the idea that marriage is permanent. For some women separation or divorce from their partner will also mean separation from their religious community. The first decision is tough in itself; feelings of failure are strong. For those women for whom separation or divorce from the partner also means the censure of or expulsion from their faith community, the decision is excruciatingly painful. The victim who seeks safety, or eventually decides to seek separation or divorce, *is* acknowledging that the covenant which she had established with another no longer exists, *but she is not the one breaking the covenant*. In fact, she is taking steps toward the basic purpose of the marriage covenant: to provide a home where the ways of life intended by God might be practiced: the ways of justice, peace, and mutual caretaking.

While marriage is a covenant that is meant to be lasting, there is nothing in scripture that can be construed to justify a lifetime of meaningless suffering, and there is substantial evidence calling for covenants with God to be ended when their purpose has been forgotten, ignored, or transgressed. Should it not be the same with covenants between people? When the marriage covenant is treated as more sacred than the way of living that it is intended to provide, are we not then abusing the very purpose of the covenant?

Conclusion

The intent of family, or marriage, covenants is to provide a place where justice, mercy, and love are lived out in keeping with God's covenantal ways. But when the family environment deviates from this intention due to the presence of abuse or violence, then the saving grace is to release the victim from the obligation. In families afflicted by domestic abuse, the only way to save the family is to allow the victim the opportunity to rededicate herself to life abundant in an environment free of the abuse.

The definition of who makes up a family is different with different cultures, circumstances, and generations. It is time we began focusing on what is really important – and that is the promise that for each of us God wishes life in all its abundance. Saving the family means ending the violence that is destroying it.

APPENDIX 2
ADDITIONAL STATISTICS ON DOMESTIC VIOLENCE*

- 95% of victims of domestic violence are women.

- There are between 2 and 4 million reported incidents of domestic violence against women every year.

- A woman is physically abused by her husband every 9 seconds in the U.S.

- Each year, 1500 women are murdered due to domestic violence.

- Up to 50% of all homeless women in the country are fleeing domestic violence.

- Domestic violence is the leading cause of injury to women age 15 to 44, more common than automobile accidents, muggings and rape combined.

- Abusive husbands and partners harass 74% of employed battered women at work, either in person or over the telephone.

- One third of all marriages endure some form of domestic abuse consistently.

- At least half of American families are affected by domestic abuse at some point.

- An estimated 3.3 million children witness their mothers being beaten.

- In 87% of violent homes, children witness the battering of their mothers.

- 70% of men who batter their female partners also abuse their children.

- The sons of the most violent parents have a rate of wife beating 10 times greater than the sons of nonviolent parents.

---

* From "*Responding to Domestic Violence: Making Changes, Bringing Hope,*" a publication of The Sabbath of Domestic Peace – An Interfaith Coalition in the Philadelphia, PA area, 2001. Used with permission.

APPENDIX 3

PREDICTORS OF DOMESTIC VIOLENCE*

The following signs often occur before actual abuse and may serve as clues to potential abuse:

1. Did he grow up in a violent family? People who grow up in families where they have been abused as children, or where one parent beats the other, have grown up learning that violence is normal behavior.

2. Does he tend to use force or violence to "solve" problems? A young man who has a criminal record for violence, who gets into fights, or who likes to act tough is likely to act the same way with his wife and children. Does he have a quick temper? Does he over-react to little problems and frustration? Is he cruel to animals? Does he punch walls or throw things when he's upset? Any of these behaviors may be a sign of a person who will work out bad feelings with violence.

3. Does he abuse alcohol or other drugs? There is a strong link between violence and problems with drugs and alcohol. Be alert to his possible drinking/drug problems, particularly if he refuses to admit that he has a problem, or refuses to get help. Do not think that you can change him.

4. Does he have strong traditional ideas about what a man should be and what a woman should be? Does he think a woman should stay at home, take care of her husband, and follow his wishes and orders?

5. Is he jealous of your other relationships – with friends (either gender) or family? Does he keep tabs on you? Does he want to know where you are at all times? Does he want you with him all of the time?

6. Does he have access to guns, knives, or other lethal instruments? Does he talk of using them against people, or threaten to use them to get even?

---

* From *General Information Packet: Every Home a Safe Home* (Denver: NCADV, 2000). Reprinted with permission of National Coalition Against Domestic Violence.

APPENDIX 3

7. Does he expect you to follow his orders or advice? Does he become angry if you do not fulfill his wishes or if you cannot anticipate what he wants?

8. Does he go through extreme highs and lows, almost as though he is two different people? Is he extremely kind one time, and extremely cruel at another time?

9. When he gets angry, do you fear him? Do you find that not making him angry has become a major part of your life? Do you do what he wants you to do, rather than what you want to do?

10. Does he treat you roughly? Does he physically force you to do what you do not want to do?

APPENDIX 4
INDICATORS THAT A MAN MAY KILL HIS PARTNER*

1. Threats of Homicide or Suicide

   The batterer who has threatened to kill himself, his partner, the children, or his partner's relatives must be considered extremely dangerous.

2. Fantasies of Homicide or Suicide

   The more the batterer has developed a fantasy about how, when, or where to kill, the more dangerous he may be. The batterer who has previously acted out part of a homicide or suicide fantasy may be invested in killing as a viable "solution" to his problems. As in suicide assessment, the more detailed the plan and the more available the method, the greater the risk.

3. Weapons

   Where a batterer possesses weapons and has used them or has threatened to use them in the past in his assaults on the battered women, the children, or himself, his access to those weapons increases his potential for lethal assault. The use of guns is a strong predictor of homicide. If a batterer has a history of arson or the threat of arson, fire should be considered a weapon.

4. "Ownership" of the battered partner

   The batterer who says "Death before divorce!" or "You belong to me and will never belong to another!" may be stating his fundamental belief that the woman has no right to life separate from him. A batterer who believes he is absolutely entitled to his female partner, her services, her obedience and her loyalty, no matter what, is likely to be life endangering.

5. Centrality of the partner

   A man who idolizes his female partner, or depends heavily on her to organize and sustain his life, or who has isolated himself from all other community, may retaliate against a partner who decides to end

---

* Adapted from Barbara Hart, "Assessing Whether Batterers Will Kill," Pennsylvania Coalition Against Domestic Violence, 1990. Used with permission.

the relationship. He rationalizes that her "betrayal" justifies his lethal retaliation.

6. Separation violence

    When a batterer believes that he is about to lose his partner, if he cannot envision life without her or if the separation causes him great despair or rage, he may choose to kill.

7. Escalation of batterer risk

    A less obvious indicator of increasing danger may be the sharp escalation of personal risk taken by the batterer; when a batterer begins to act without regard to the legal or social consequences that previously constrained his violence, chances of lethal assault increase significantly.

8. Hostage-taking

    A hostage-taker is at high risk of inflicting homicide. Between 75 percent and 90 percent of all hostage takings in the United States are related to domestic violence situations.

9. Depression

    Where a batterer has been acutely depressed and sees little hope for moving beyond the depression, he may be a candidate for homicide and suicide. Research shows that many men who are hospitalized for depression have homicidal fantasies directed at family members.

10. Repeated outreach to law enforcement

    Partner or spousal homicide almost always occurs in a context of historical violence. Prior calls to the police indicate elevated risk of life-threatening conduct.

11. Access to the battered woman or to family members

    If the batterer cannot find her, he cannot kill her. If he does not have access to the children, he cannot use them as a means of access to the battered woman. Careful safety planning and police assistance are required for those times when contact is required, for example, court appearances and custody exchanges.

APPENDIX 5

ACCOUNTABILITY*

A man who has battered a woman becomes accountable when:

1. He has acknowledged to the battered woman and to their community of friends that he has assaulted and controlled a woman, and that he has committed acts of violence against her.

2. He has admitted the pattern of abusive control that tyrannized her.

3. He recognizes that his behavior was unprovoked and inexcusable.

4. He knows his behavior was criminal.

5. He understands his behavior was not caused by stress, chemical dependency, or any other outside factor.

6. He knows he was not out of control.

7. He admits that he intended to control or punish her.

8. He deeply regrets his actions and is horrified.

9. He recognizes the pain and suffering he visited upon her.

10. He accepts full responsibility for his acts.

11. He acknowledges this without expectations of approval from her.

12. He understands he is not entitled to her forgiveness.

13. He recognizes that the woman may never trust him again and may remain afraid of him forever.

14. He can enumerate the losses suffered by her and her family.

15. He does not expect protection for his name.

---

* Adapted from Barbara Hart, "Assessing Whether Batterers Will Kill," Pennsylvania Coalition Against Domestic Violence, 1990. Used with permission.

APPENDIX 5

16. He realizes he needs the help of his family, his friends, and his community to prevent further use of violence.

17. He knows that he needs to find others to support him in nonviolence.

18. He knows clearly that there is nothing in the relationship of the woman that caused his battery.

19. He knows he is at risk of battering any woman in the future.

20. He realizes that the battered woman should not have to hear any of the above points from him, unless she desires to hear it.

21. He agrees to limit contact with her, her friends, and her family.

22. He agrees to stop chasing and tracking her.

23. He agrees to avoid the places she frequents and to provide her with plenty of space away from him.

24. He agrees to stop collecting information about her.

25. He understands he needs to pay restitution, which could mean child support or alimony if she desires, and he agrees to support her in this restitution as long as she needs it, to replace the losses she has sustained.

26. He refuses to manipulate their children to discredit her.

APPENDIX 6

RESOURCES COMMONLY USED IN PREMARITAL COUNSELING

The following are some programmatic or published resources sometimes used by pastors and therapists in conjunction with their own creative efforts to provide quality premarital counseling. This is far from a complete list. Several denominations have excellent resources as well. Our hope here is to name a few of these resources that include the topic of domestic violence in a direct and useful manner.

1. Premarital Assessment Questionnaires (PAQs)

In each of the following commonly used instruments, the responsibility for identifying current or potential domestic violence resides with the professional person who administers and interprets the instrument. Some assessment questionnaires include direct questions related to domestic violence; others access the desired information through indirect topics (communications, family history, values, etc.). Both approaches assume a skilled and trained professional will follow up to explore the topic in greater depth. All of these tools involve a cost to the couple and all provide supplemental materials for couples to use in future relationship work.

- **Premarital Preparation and Relationship Enhancement (PREPARE)** - developed in 1968 by Dr. David H. Olson of the University of Minnesota in St. Paul, President of Life Innovations; revised numerous times, most recently in 1996. It has 195 questions in eleven content areas. PREPARE has components for couples at differing relationship stages (e.g., pre-marriage to re-marriage, with or without children, cohabiting or not, over 50 years of age, etc). It was designed to identify and measure premarital "relationship strengths" and "work areas" and to collect "comprehensive data relevant to the premarital counseling or education process." Professionals in the field of pastoral counseling or mental health who are trained to use this instrument administer it. It is available in six foreign languages as well as English. (www.lifeinnovations.com)

APPENDIX 6

- **Facilitating Open Couple Communication, Understanding and Study (FOCCUS)** – developed by Barbara Markey, Ph.D., Director of Family Life Office for the Archdiocese of Omaha and Associate Director of the Research Center for Marriage and Family at Creighton University. Originally designed for use in Roman Catholic premarital preparation courses, it has been revised and is now available in four editions: General, Christian Nondenominational, Catholic, and Alternate (for learning impaired) couples. It is not intended to be a predictor of success or failure in marriage; rather, it is "a tool to help couples name and work through issues before marriage." This instrument (consisting of 156 basic items and more depending on the couple's situation) is designed to be used at three levels: 1) Couples read and respond to the FOCCUS statements and discuss what they think and feel about the topics. 2) A facilitator helps the couple look at patterns and issues which have surfaced in the FOCCUS instrument. 3) The couple is referred to a pre-marriage group program to practice communication skills, etc. or to more focused work on a particular topic with a therapist as determined by the facilitator. A couple receives a personalized profile summarizing their areas of agreements and areas for discussion for further work in the premarital process. Available in several languages. (www.foccusinc.com)

- **RELATionship Evaluation (RELATE)** – created by the Marriage Study Consortium (comprised of scholars, researchers, family life educators, and counselors from varied religious and educational backgrounds) at Brigham Young University in 1980, with changes added through the years.

    Partners answer 276 questions and receive a report showing areas of strength and weakness in the relationship, a graph showing the ratings partners gave for themselves and their partners, interpretations of how childhood experiences have shaped their current personalities, and suggestions for how to improve the relationship. RELATE is available online for couples or individuals to take alone and it is intended to be sufficiently comprehensive to guide therapists and professionals from many disciplines in assessing couple patterns, problem areas, and the risk for separation or divorce. (www.relate-institute.org)

- **Pre-Marital Inventory (PMI)** – This inventory workbook (Sayers and Burnett, Intercommunications Publishing Inc.) of 140 agree/disagree statements is filled out by both partners. After it is scored, a printed profile is shared and interpreted with the couple by a trained pastor/professional. There are several places where "red flags" related to potential or actual domestic violence are noted. In addition, the final profile offers a clear list of issues recommended for continued couple attention. (www.Intercompub.com)

2. *Nationally based premarital programs*

- **Prevention and Relationship Enhancement Program (PREP)** – founded by Howard Markman, PhD and Scott Stanley, PhD of the Center for Marital and Family Studies at the University of Denver. This program – developed for both secular and Christian audiences – has been used in over 50 countries. Clergy, mental health professionals and lay leaders are trained to administer and lead it. The intent of the program is educational, not therapeutic. Leaders present core themes in brief lectures. (www.prepinc.com)

- **Evenings for the Engaged** – This program, developed by Fr. Chuck Gallagher, S.J. (founder of Worldwide Marriage Encounter and the Pastoral and Matrimonial Renewal Center) utilizes couple discussions, written exercises and group discussion based on topics raised in a format which involves trained married couples as leaders. Usually based in local churches, married couples are trained as Facilitator Couples. Using a Leader's Guide written by Jim and Paula Dahl and Fr. Gallagher, they then lead six evening sessions in their own homes for a small group of engaged couples. A Couple Pak provides appealing, engaging focus on many topics, including domestic violence. (Contact your local Roman Catholic Archdiocese for times and location in your area.)

- **Engaged Encounter** – The design of this program is similar throughout the country under the guidance of many different Protestant denominations and the Roman Catholic Church. Engaged couples attend a full weekend gathering at a retreat location. Three married couples (and clergy) present wisdom and information about many topics to the whole group. Engaged couples then have a time to write and discuss their thoughts related to the topic just presented. The aim of this program is to cover dimensions which are thought to be important in preparing for a lifetime covenant commitment. (Contact your local denominational office for specific times and places in your area.)

- **Great Start** – A program designed to help couples prepare realistically for marriage and prevent divorce by building a skilled, happy and growing relationship. It is based on and includes resources from two well known national programs: PREPARE/ENRICH (Life Innovations, Inc.) and COUPLE COMMUNICATION (Interpersonal Communications Programs, Inc.). The process of workbooks, inventories, classes and evaluation takes place over a two-year period (before marriage and one year later) and is led by trained clergy or counselors. Current or potential domestic violence is revealed by numerous couple responses which the counselor/pastor is trained to identify throughout the process. (www.lifeinnovations.com)

3. Self-directed workbooks

Couples can purchase and use the following or these can be used in a mentoring relationship in a local church, when one married couple agrees to work with one engaged couple. They may also be used in a group setting of several engaged couples.

- **Saving Your Marriage Before It Starts** – Parrott, Les and Parrott, Leslie, 1995, Zondervan Press, Grand Rapids, Michigan.

  Co-founders (in 1991) of the Center for Relationship Development at Seattle Pacific University in Seattle, Wa., this clinical psychologist and marriage and family therapist couple provides an accessible and provocative book for engaged couples or groups of couples. Topics include communication blocks and aids, exploring the myth of marriage, and affirming the spiritual component of marital commitment, among others. Helpful and practical suggestions are offered for couple use.

- **A Decision to Love** – Marriage Preparation Program, John M.V. Midgley and Susan Vollmer Midgley, 1998 Seventh Printing, Twenty-Third Publications

  This resource includes a couple's workbook and a leader's guide. In the couple's workbook, domestic violence is named in several places with rare directness: "If physical abuse is already present in your relationship, then call off the wedding now! Things will not get better. They will get worse." Action steps are then given to direct partners to appropriate support resources.

APPENDIX 6

- **Preparing for Marriage: A Guide for Christian Couples** – Edited by Donald J. Luther, Augsburg Fortress Press, Minneapolis, MN, 1992

    Edited by a Lutheran pastor, this collection of worksheets and exercises is intended to help couples have important conversations. This resource can also be used by a pastor with a couple. It includes clear and direct attention to domestic violence.

- **Now Bring Your Joy to This Wedding …Couples in Premarital Preparation** – Norma S. Wood and Lisa M. Leber, CSS Publishing Co, Inc., Lima, Ohio, copyright 2002

    In a three ring binder, exercises and text are intertwined with Biblical passages in six topical chapters in this Lutheran resource. Domestic violence is addressed straightforwardly and helpfully.

- **Growing in Faith, United in Love** – Barb Nardi Kurtz, Discipleship Resources, Nashville, TN, copyright 1998

    This small book is intended to help married couples enhance their covenantal relationships with each other and with God. The author gathered stories from twenty couples to inform and inspire her writing. It can be used by couples alone, in support groups or church classes, or with a pastor or counselor. The topics and process are also relevant for engaged couples.

4. *Local premarital programs*

Many local campus ministries, therapists, churches, a consortium of churches, or counseling agencies offer premarital programs in their geographical areas. If you are lucky enough to live near a seminary, you may find that courses addressing pastoral care and domestic violence are available for your continuing education. If such a course is not offered, ask for one. More and more seminaries are recognizing that this dimension of pastoral care should be an essential part of the curriculum and are offering excellent courses for students.

Individual therapists often use other resources, such as the Genogram, the Myers Briggs Type Indicator, or the Taylor Johnson Temperament Analysis, along with their own counseling strategies, to reveal present or potential domestic violence. It is wise to use the criteria found in Chapter Four for screening the best and most appropriate resource for you. Interviewing therapists about their particular approaches to premarital counseling related to the criteria is also encouraged.

APPENDIX 7

Excerpts from "Counseling the Clergy on How to Help Victims of Domestic Violence" by SaraKay Smullens, M.S.W., B.C.D., Founder of Sabbath of Domestic Peace, Philadelphia, PA*

1. Effective Clergy Counseling

   We urge religious leaders to keep in mind that a clergyman/woman may be the first person an abused woman talks to about her situation. We advise them to recognize that it is difficult for a woman to acknowledge that she is a victim of abuse. She may not label what happens to her at home as abuse; instead, she may talk about her partner being upset or things not going well at home. We advise clergy to listen to what they are told, believe what they hear, and understand that women may be embarrassed, confused, or ambivalent about what they are experiencing. We also ask clergy to be aware that it usually takes time for an abused partner to be able to leave a marriage. We ask them to communicate that no one deserves to be hurt and that the parishioner's safety and that of their children are of deep concern. We ask that they tell victims of abuse that they are not alone and that help is available. We stress that a woman should be asked if it is safe for her to go home, and, if not, whether she has a place to go. In addition, we advise that she be told about the need for a thorough plan for leaving --- when to go, whom to call and whom not call, what to take, and so on. Further, she needs to be provided with an updated list of resources available to help her. Above all, we advise against suggesting joint marriage counseling because this can be dangerous until the violence has stopped and a woman is safe; an abused woman who speaks openly in counseling sessions with her partner is in danger of being assaulted following a session, as are her children.

---

* From *Annals of the American Psychotherapy Association*, November/December 2001. Used with permission.

2. Myths and Realities of Domestic Abuse and Violence

We communicate the most common myths about domestic abuse and their corresponding realities:

Myth: Women enjoy being abused.
Reality: No one enjoys being abused.

Myth: What happens in the home is private. Outsiders should not get involved.
Reality: Turning away from abuse in a home is tantamount to condoning violence. Ending domestic abuse is everyone's responsibility.

Myth: Women invent or exaggerate stories of abuse.
Reality: An abused woman is very reluctant to come forward and reveal what has happened to her. When she does get the courage to reach out for help, she must be believed.

Myth: Women are to blame; they provoke domestic violence.
Reality: A woman's behavior is not a cause or an excuse for violence.

Myth: Domestic violence is a problem only among the poor and minority groups.
Reality: Domestic violence happens in all cultures, races, and classes.

Myth: Financial security stops domestic violence.
Reality: Domestic violence occurs at all socioeconomic levels.

Myth: Abusers are violent toward everyone, everywhere.
Reality: Abusers may be charming, helpful, and kind to those with whom they work or with whom they are involved in the community. Their abuse may occur only in their homes.

Myth: Marriage stops the abuse.
Reality: Violence escalates when an abuser marries.

Myth: Rape cannot happen in marriage.
Reality: When one is forced to engage in sexual acts against her or his will, a rape has occurred.

Myth: Prayer and faith alone will stop the abuse.
Reality: Prayer and faith alone will not stop the abuse.

Myth: Any woman could leave an abusive situation if she really wanted to.
Reality: Leaving an abuser is a very complicated process.

APPENDIX 7

Myth: Abusive partners will always abuse.
Reality: The "honeymoon phase" of domestic violence should not be confused with a de-escalation of violence. However, with the right combination of counseling or therapy, commitment, determination, hard work, and community support, it is possible to change abusive patterns.

3. Why Women Stay

In discussing the question of why women stay, we concentrate on their fear, the risks of their leaving, their lack of economic resources, their physical and emotional isolation, their commitment to their partners, and their hope for change. We also address their confidence in the value of counseling for the abuser, which is a long and difficult challenge and only effective when a full commitment is made to a process that is exceedingly painful. We also address the problems of societal denial of domestic abuse, religious and cultural pressures to keep a family intact, the immobilizing impact of shame and humiliation, and the misguided belief that any father in the home, even an abusive one, is better than no father at all.

APPENDIX 8
RESPONDING TO DOMESTIC VIOLENCE: GUIDELINES FOR CLERGY*

Remember the Goals:

1. SAFETY for the woman and children

2. ACCOUNTABILITY for the abuser

3. RESTORATION of individuals and, IF POSSIBLE, relationships

   OR

   MOURNING the loss of the relationships

DOs and DON'Ts with a battered woman

DO believe her. Her description of the violence is only the tip of the iceberg.

DO reassure her that this is not her fault, she doesn't deserve this treatment, it is not God's will for her.

DO give her referral information; primary resources are battered women's services or shelters and National Hotline. 1-800-799-SAFE (7233) 1-800-787-3224 (TDD)

DO support and respect her choices. Even if she is aware of the risks and chooses initially to return to the abuser, it is her choice. She has the most information about how to survive.

DO encourage her to think about a safety plan: set aside some money; copies of important papers for her and the children and a change of clothes hidden or

* © 2006 FaithTrust Institute. Used with permission.

in care of a friend if she decides to go to a shelter. Plan how to exit the house the next time the abuser is violent. Plan what to do about the children if they are at school, if they are asleep, etc. (This is both practical and helps her stay in touch with the reality of the abuser's violence. Safety planning is a process that is ongoing.)

DO protect her confidentiality. DO NOT give information about her or her whereabouts to the abuser or to others who might pass information on to the abuser. Do not discuss her situation with the parish council/session/elders who might inadvertently pass information on to the abuser.

DO help her with any religious concerns. If she is Christian, give her a copy of *Keeping the Faith: Guidance for Christial Women Facing Abuse*. Refer to www.faithtrustinstitute.org for copies of this book and other helpful information.

DO emphasize that the marriage covenant is broken by the violence from her partner. DO assure her of God's love and presence, of your commitment to walk with her through this valley of the shadow of death.

DO help her see that her partner's violence has broken the marriage covenant and that God does not want her to remain in a situation where her life and the lives of her children are in danger.

If she decides to separate and divorce, DO support her and help her to mourn the loss to herself and her children.

DO pray with her. Ask God to give her the strength and courage she needs.

DON'T minimize the danger to her. You can be a reality check. "From what you have told me, I am very much concerned for your safety . . ."

DON'T tell her what to do. Give information and support.

DON'T react with disbelief, disgust, or anger at what she tells you. But don't react passively either. Let her know that you are concerned and that what the abuser has done to her is wrong and not deserved by her.

DON'T blame her for his violence. If she is blaming herself, try to reframe: "I don't care if you did have supper late or forget to water the lawn, that is no reason for him to be violent with you. This is his problem."

APPENDIX 8

DON'T recommend couples' counseling or approach her husband and ask for "his side of the story." These actions will endanger her.

DON'T recommend "marriage enrichment," "mediation," or a "communications workshop." None of these will address the goals listed above.

DON'T send her home with just a prayer and directive to submit to her husband, bring him to church, or be a better Christian wife.

DON'T encourage her to forgive him and take him back.

DO NOT encourage her dependence on you OR BECOME EMOTIONALLY OR SEXUALLY INVOLVED WITH HER.

DON'T do nothing.

DO consult with colleagues in the wider community who may have expertise and be able to assist you in your response. Refer to www.faithtrustinstitute.org for resources.

DOs and DON'Ts with an abusive partner

If he has been arrested, DO approach him and express your concern and support for him to be accountable and to deal with his violence.

DON'T meet with him alone and in private. Meet in a public place or in the church with several other people around.

DON'T approach him or let him know that you know about his violence unless a) you have the victim's permission, b) she is aware that you plan to talk to him and c) you are certain that his partner is safely separated from him.

DO address any religious rationalizations he may offer or questions he may have. DON'T allow him to use religious excuses for his behavior.

DO name the violence as his problem, not hers. Tell him that only he can stop it; and you are willing to help.

DO refer him to a program which specifically addresses abusers.

DO assess him for suicide or threats of homicide. DO warn the victim if he makes specific threats towards her.

DON'T pursue couples' counseling with him and his partner if you are aware that there is violence in the relationship.

DON'T go to him to confirm the victim's story.

DON'T give him any information about his partner or her whereabouts.

DON'T be taken in by his minimization, denial or lying about his violence. DON'T accept his blaming her or other rationalizations for his behavior.

DON'T be taken in by his "conversion" experience. If it is genuine, it will be a tremendous resource as he proceeds with accountability. If it is phony, it is only another way to manipulate you and the system and maintain control of the process to avoid accountability.

DON'T advocate for the abuser to avoid the legal consequences of his violence.

DON'T provide a character witness for this purpose in any legal proceedings.

DON'T forgive an abuser quickly and easily. DON'T confuse his remorse with true repentance.

DON'T send him home with just a prayer. Work with others in the community to hold him accountable.

DO pray with him. Ask God to help him stop his violence, repent and find a new way. DO assure him of your support in this endeavor.

DO find ways to collaborate with community agencies and law enforcement to hold him accountable.

For information addressing religion and abuse, refer to www.faithtrustinstitute.org.

APPENDIX 9
RELIGIOUS COMMUNITY: A COMMUNITY CHECKLIST*

The religious communities provide a safe haven for women and families in need. In addition, they exhort society to share compassion and comfort with those afflicted by the tragedy of domestic violence. Leaders of the religious community have identified actions to create a unified response to violence against women.

- *Become a Safe Place.* Make your church, temple, mosque or synagogue a safe place where victims of domestic violence can come for help. Display brochures and posters which include the telephone number of the domestic violence and sexual assault programs in your area. Publicize the National Domestic Violence Hotline number, 1-800-799-SAFE (7233) or 1-800-787-3224 (TDD).

- *Educate the Congregation.* Provide ways for members of the congregation to learn as much as they can about domestic and sexual violence. Routinely include information in monthly newsletters, on bulletin boards, and in marriage preparation classes. Sponsor educational seminars on violence against women in your congregation.

- *Speak Out.* Speak out about domestic violence and sexual assault from the pulpit. As a faith leader, you can have a powerful impact on people's attitudes and beliefs.

- *Lead by Example.* Volunteer to serve on the board of directors at the local domestic violence/sexual assault program or attend a training to become a crisis volunteer.

- *Offer Space.* Offer meeting space for educational seminars or weekly support groups or serve as a supervised visitation site when parents need to safely visit their children.

---

* Adapted from the Nebraska Domestic Violence and Sexual Assault Coalition. Used with permission.

- *Partner with Existing Resources.* Include your local domestic violence or sexual assault program in donations and community service projects. Adopt a shelter for which your church, temple, mosque or synagogue provides material support, or provide similar support to families as they rebuild their lives following a shelter stay.

- *Prepare to be a Resource.* Do the theological and scriptural homework necessary to better understand and respond to family violence and receive training from professionals in the fields of sexual and domestic violence.

- *Intervene.* If you suspect violence is occurring in a relationship, speak to each member of the couple separately. Help the victim plan for safety. Let both individuals know of the community resources available to assist them. Do not attempt couples' counseling.

- *Support Professional Training.* Encourage and support training and education for clergy and lay leaders, hospital chaplains, and seminary students to increase awareness about sexual and domestic violence.

- *Address Internal Issues.* Encourage continued efforts by religious institutions to address allegations of abuse by religious leaders to insure that religious leaders are a safe resource for victims and their children.

ABOUT THE WRITERS

SUSAN YARROW MORRIS has built her life and work on the concept of Covenant. Having grown up in a family which often welcomed strangers into its midst, she, with her husband and son, shared life for sixteen years in an intentional covenantal community on Whidbey Island, WA. In her professional career, she has taught and inspired others to explore the strength, depth and power of covenantal relationships, whether between two persons or in larger groups.

During her sixteen years as Campus Pastor at the ecumenical Campus Christian Ministry at the University of Washington, she founded and directed the Marriage Preparation Program. She continued this and the development of other small group initiatives as Minister of Parish Life and Care at Plymouth Congregational United Church of Christ, and subsequently as Associate and Marriage Minister at Fauntleroy Church UCC, both in Seattle, WA.

She is an ordained minister in the United Church of Christ. Now retired from fulltime parish ministry, Susan continues to be a retreat leader, speaker and preacher. She serves as Liturgical Consultant to UCC students at Seattle University's School of Theology and Ministry. She is active on various committees and ventures of the United Church of Christ as well as in the ecumenical community.

JEAN ANTON has been working in the movement to end violence against women and children for over 25 years. She has been on the staff of FaithTrust Institute for 21 years and has served as Executive Producer of more than 10 award-winning videos, including *Not In My Church, Broken Vows, To Save a Life, Love-All That and More,* and *A Sacred Trust.* She is a practicing Theravadan Buddhist and is deeply committed to integrating spiritual practice with social change work.

This project was supported by Grant No. 2004-WT-BX-K032 awarded by the Office on Violence Against Women, Office of Justice Programs, U.S. Department of Justice. Points of view in this document are those of the author and do not necessarily represent the official position or policies of the U.S. Department of Justice.

www.ingramcontent.com/pod-product-compliance
Lightning Source LLC
Chambersburg PA
CBHW081328190426
43193CB00044B/2890